Experiencing the Beacon Within

A Guide to Lead You Back to Your Authentic Self

Reverend Dr. Ron Fox

Experiencing the Beacon Within
A Guide to Lead You Back to Your Authentic Self
By Reverend Dr. Ron Fox

Copyright © 2020 Reverend Dr. Ron Fox

All Rights Reserved. No part of this book may be reproduced or transmitted in any form or by any means, electronic or mechanical, including photocopying, faxing, recording, emailing, posting on social media or by an information storage and retrieval system, or used for any other purpose without written permission from the author.

Published by Blue Spruce Publishing
2175 Golf Isle Drive, Suite 1024
Melbourne, Florida USA 32935
610.647.8863
info@BlueSprucePublishing.com

Cover Design: Becky Fox | Email: innervsion@gmail.com
Cover Photo: Greg Rakozy - Unsplash
Author Photo: Gregory Carr
Graphics Before Each Section: Becky Fox

ISBN: 978-1-943581-23-8

Table of Contents

A Dedication to My Father	i
Forward	iii
Introduction	v
Acknowledgements	vii
Endorsements	viii
Daily Guides	**1**
Tell It Like It Could Be	3
Live for Today	4
Living a Limitless Life	5
Your Life as a Gift	6
You are the One	7
Staying Centered in Difficult Times	8
No Quick Fix	9
The Myth of Perfection	10
What Do You Expect	11
The Open Door	12
Counting Our Blessings	13
The Beauty of a New Day	14
Life Goes On	15
This is What I Know	16
Stepping Into the Unknown	17
Standing in Your Truth	18
Walking Through Fear	19
Reconciliation: Moving Past the Hurt	20
The Power of Choice	21
The Humble Servant	22
Choosing Peace	23

We Are More than Our Differences	24
The Gifts of Community	25
Being Real	26
A Time for Renewal	27
Back to Basics	28
Spiritual Resilience	29
Beginning Anew	30
Healing Power	31
Opening to Our Abundance	32
The Hidden Blessings in Obstacles	33
Oneness	34
Unlocking Our Unlimited Potential	35
Accepting What Is	36
Forgiveness	37
Courting the Presence	38
Living a Legacy	39
The Challenge of Faith	40
Why Do We Suffer?	41
Being Receptive	42
We Are One	43
Discover Your Spiritual Power	44
How to See Yourself as You Really Are	45
Self-Mastery	46
Honoring All People	47
Transcending Fear	48
Different World Views: What to do	49
Living in Integrity	50
Living a Spiritual Life	51
Going Through Difficult Times	52
Embracing Change	53
Change Your Thinking and See the Results	54

Purpose, Power & Passion	55
Living in Uncertain Times	56
Moving From Fear to Faith	57
The Pearl Principle	58
Anticipation	59
Christmas Unwrapped	60
Getting Your Life to Hum	61
The Way of the Mystic	62
Healing and Prayer	63
Opening to Our Abundance	64
Centering in Truth	65
A Call to Renewal	66
The Power of Believing	67
Graduation	68
Illuminations	**69**
A Ring and a Prayer	71
Blessings Abound	73
Feeling Abundant	75
Giving Thanks	77
It Really Works	79
Looking Within	80
Opening to our Abundance	81
Quiet Time	83
Remembering What Is Important	85
Resilience	87
Seeing Beyond Appearances	89
Starting Over	91
The Book	93
The Gift of Stillness	95
The Greatest Gift	97

The Move	99
There Is Always Enough	101
Unexpected Income	103
We Are More Than Our Differences	105
Wilbur	107
You Are a Spiritual Powerhouse	109
You Make the Choice	111
What We Want Wants Us	113
Affirmations	**115**
Oneness	117
Love	119
Choice	121
Courage	123
Sacred Journey	125
Power	127
Change	129
Additional Affirmations	131
Author Bio and Contact Info	**133**

A Dedication to My Father
Be What You Wish

It is a weekend morning many years ago; a young boy sits with his dad listening to the radio. Sometimes they sing along with the music, sometimes they just listen. More often than not, the radio is just a vehicle for the father to spend time with the son he loves so much. Life hasn't been kind to the dad, his dream of being a doctor died when the money ran out and his wealthy cousin said no when he asked for a loan. He married late in life and the marriage isn't good. He and his wife argue all the time and sometimes the fights get physical. Unfortunately, his life and his dreams never met.

If there is anything in his life that still shines it is the love he has for the only child the marriage produced. The world begins and ends with his boy. These weekend mornings mean so much to him, he desperately wants his son to live the dream he never did or could. So, he uses this time together to talk about the life this young boy could have. "You are so smart. You can have it all. Go to law school, be writer, work hard and go to college, don't blow it like I did. The world is your oyster."

The boy loved his father too, and he listened and worked hard and went to college, got a good job, married and had children. But something was missing, the big dreams he had, always seemed out of reach. He had a good life, but not the one he had dreamed about. Then as it seems to do so often history repeated itself, the marriage went south, the dreams were shattered and life was empty. But our story doesn't end here; sometimes the worst of times can give birth to the best of times.

They came from different worlds; she had never been east of Wyoming he grew up in New York. She was quiet and shy, he was a wiseass. She hardly knew her father, he idolized his. But below the surface they shared a dream, they each wanted more from life, they each were sure they had more to offer life and that was enough to bond them. Reluctantly at first, she went back to her art. She was better than ever. Her talent had matured. She saw something in him he had lost years ago. "You are a great writer, write something." So, he did, he wrote and was published and even got paid for it.

Creativity is so fragile. It doesn't take much to wound or injure it. A passing word, a snide comment, and like a turtle, it retreats into its shell to wait for another day. But fragile isn't weak and so an encouraging word, a smile, a pat on the back and out it comes again. What we came here to do must be done, and so barriers must be taken down, limits must be passed, and comfort zones broadened.

And so today, the once young boy looks back on a man who loved him enough to encourage him to be everything that he could be, and in his heart says, "Thank you, you set the stage for me." And he looks straight ahead at the woman he loves and says, "Thank you for reminding me of who I could be, and that taking a risk is easier than living with what could have been."

Forward

When Rev. Dr. Ron Fox asked me to write the forward to his book, I was honored. You are in for a great ride. Rev. Dr. Ron Fox and I have been friends for over ten years, first meeting at a United Centers for Spiritual Living (now called Centers for Spiritual Living), Convention in 2008, in Anaheim, CA. He was a Minister of one of the member churches, and I was, at the time, the Program Coordinator at Home Office for United Centers for Spiritual Living in the Department World Ministry of Prayer. Our first meeting was pleasant, nothing to write home about. However, as time went by, Rev. Dr. Ron and I became more than colleagues spreading the teachings of Science of Mind and Spirit. We became good friends.

One of the things that brought Ron and I together was we both wrote articles and the Daily Guides for the Science of Mind Magazine. If you are not familiar with this publication, I invite you check it out. It is filled with articles that can and will change your life.

Being published authors for the Science of Mind Magazine strengthened our connection, which I believe is what prompted Rev. Dr. Ron to invite me to facilitate a workshop for his community in Florida. This is when I realized that we were kindred souls. Hosted by him, and his best friend and lovely wife Becky, who is also a powerful Religious Science Practitioner, I got a chance to see who Ron Fox really was. Not just Rev. Dr. Ron Fox, the minister of a Religious Science Center in Florida. I got to see the heart and soul of the man.

During that weekend Ron and I shared some deep conversations, light-hearted bantering, laughter, good food, and some tears. We found that our paths were closely related, sharing some of the hurts and pains that bring many of us to this teaching. I consider Ron Fox a true friend. And as friends, Ron and I created a space where we both could share from the depths of our hearts. This is what you are holding in your hands, a piece of Ron's heart.

The book you are holding right now can be a gateway that can change your life. It is a gateway into a deeper consciousness, your deeper consciousness. An awareness of the power and the presence that resides in you and shows up in the world as you.

Rev. Moira Fox, another Centers for Spiritual Living minister once said to me: "You know Eugene, a person doesn't have to tell you whether or not they are doing their prayer work, you can tell by how they live their lives."

Yep, this is Rev. Dr. Ron Fox. This is his way of life. He has a clear understanding of the principles of the Science of Mind and Spirit. He has a firm grasp on the power of prayer. You can tell by how he lives his life. Ron is not just one of those individuals who goes around saying that "It's All Good" just for the sake of saying it. Like I said, we have shared some deep tears. But it is the way that he uses these principles to bring him back to center that shines so brightly. Rev. Dr. Ron knows firsthand that life may throw some curve balls, and shucks, that's life. However, there are tools that he uses that brings him back to center.

I am grateful that Rev. Dr. Ron Fox was guided to share what he knows about these tools with us and the world. This is what you are holding in your hand - guidebook that can guide you back to your center, back to your authentic self.

In Deep Heartfelt Gratitude,
Eugene D. Holden, RScP

INTRODUCTION

For more than twenty years I have had the privilege to write for Science of Mind Magazine. During that time, I have written feature articles, guides for daily living, and a column on practical prosperity. I have enjoyed every minute of that time.

For the past several years many of my friends have been encouraging me to put some of the writings into a book. *Experiencing the Beacon Within* is the result of that encouragement. Here you will find a smattering of the guides, my columns (Illuminations), and a separate section of affirmations.

My fondest wish is that readers will use this material as an inspiration in living their daily lives. I have included quotes from some great thinkers, stories that I hope will inspire and affirmations that can be used as a tool for positive reinforcement of issues we may be facing in our life.

For readers who may not be familiar with the Centers for Spiritual Living, below is an explanation of some terms I use throughout the book.

Ernest Holmes was a philosopher, writer and teacher who founded the philosophy known as Religious Science.

Religious Science is a religious movement that is found within the New Thought movement. The term Religious Science applies to the organization. The term Science of Mind applies to the teaching. The organization has also become known as the Centers for Spiritual Living.

Centers for Spiritual Living is a practical spiritual teaching that draws on the wisdom of the ages and New Thought principles, in order to promote awakening and personal growth.

Prayer Treatment describes a form of affirmative prayer, used as a tool to assist us in changing our mind about appearances. There are five steps in prayer treatment they are: recognition, unification, realization, thanksgiving and release. A fuller description can be found in the book, *It Is About You*, by Kathy Juline.

Foundation Class is where we discuss the principles and practices of what we believe. Some of the topics we cover are: prayer, meditation, grace, and immortality.

Practitioner is someone who undertakes a rigorous two year course of study. At the completion of the two years the practitioner is licensed to meet with people and do spiritual counseling, assist the minister on the platform, pray with people who need prayer work and teach classes.

As I say in the book, I believe that we all have the power to create the life of our choosing. We are all spiritual power houses. By using some very simple and easy to understand principles we can be the masters of our fate. So, as you read the material know that it is written to help you grow personally and spiritually, and to transform your life.

Marcel Proust reminds us, "The voyage of discovery lies not in finding new landscapes, but in having new eyes." I hope dear reader that the material in this book is a guide in helping you to find those new eyes, and remembering that wherever you are God is right beside you on the great journey we call life.

Reverend Dr. Ron Fox

ACKNOWLEDGMENTS

Writing a book is a team effort. My name is on the cover but there are so many more people who without their guidance and effort this book would not be a reality.

Rosemary Augustine, my publisher, has been a source of encouragement, advice and friendship. Her hand is on every page of this work and I can't thank her enough for her guidance and patience.

There are so many friends that have encouraged me to write this book and have given me guidance support throughout the years. Time and space and a poor memory will not let me remember everyone but here are a few of the people who have been instrumental in my writing career.

Linda McNamar, Mary Louise Ruffner, and Nancy Berggren have been friends and mentors since my days in ministerial school.

Roger and Kathy Juline and Yolanda Porter have given me encouragement and editorial help all through this project and so many others. They have all made me a better writer.

Patt Perkins has been a friend and teacher for over twenty years. Her love and friendship have made me a better person for which I will always be indebted to her.

Jenna Watkins, my sister from another mother, has been a source of encouragement in my writing and my life.

Lastly, for over thirty years the guiding light in my life has been my wife Becky. She has been my teacher, my friend, my lover and a source of constant encouragement in everything I do. There are no words to describe the love and gratitude I have for what she has meant to me.

To all those who have encouraged me whether your name is on this page or not thank you for being in my life and a source of love and light for me. I give thanks for all of you every day.

ENDORSEMENTS

This beautiful offering of meditations of the heart, spiritual affirmations and insightful messages of practical spirituality, is sure to awaken a new generation of truth seekers to a brand new way of being in the world. The seasoned lover of life may dive even deeper into the fulfillment of self-realization. Each theme welcomes a brand-new day of hope, faith, and courage. Thank you, Rev. Dr. Ron, for this inspiration.

Rev. Mary Louise Ruffner, Co-Founder/Director of StillPoint Spiritual Center

I have known Rev. Dr. Ron Fox for many years as a friend and a writer. He is one of those people who puts spiritual principles into action in his daily life. I think that is what brings his writing right into the heart. Ron cares for people in a deep way whether they are friends and family or the unknown reader he has not met. It is easy to apply to our everyday experiences what Rev. Dr. Ron has written, creating a more positive, joyful experience for all of us. What a wonderful person and I am proud to call him a long-time friend and colleague.

Rev. Dr. Linda McNamar, Laguna Woods Center for Spiritual Living, Laguna Woods, California

Meditations don't get better than this. This book contains many inspiring aphorisms and condensed lessons. Rev. Dr. Ron makes this the perfect daily companion for yourself or a friend.

Rev. Dr. Patt Perkins

In this book, Rev. Dr. Ron Fox shares his spiritual insights through personal stories and observations in an informal and entertaining way. His successful experience in ministry and life gives him the wisdom to open all of us to a deeper understanding of spiritual principles and their application. We recommend this book to any who seek a more meaningful sense of how the inner Divinity expresses in the outer world.

Rev. Dr. Roger Juline and Kathy Juline, RScP

Eighteen years ago, Rev. Dr. Ron Fox introduced me to the principles of Science of Mind. His gifted writings on Practical Prosperity and his Daily Guides in the Science of Mind Magazines throughout the years have been great guidance. His inspirations of wisdom, love and Truth have led me to learn how to accept and enjoy all the blessings that life has to offer.

Shari Howard Teal - RScP Candidate in Training

Rev. Dr. Ron Fox was our #1 favorite guest speaker at the Fallbrook Center for Spiritual Living in California, when I was the senior minister there. His easy-going style made it possible for our community members to grasp the deep spiritual principles he taught with warmth and humor. Rev. Dr. Ron is the real deal, and the contributions he has made over the years to the Science of Mind Magazine are truly outstanding and inspiring. Each one deeply thought through and presented in a way that moves our souls and warms our hearts. A friend, colleague, leader of CSL and brilliant advocate for the teachings of Ernest Holmes and other great New Thought leaders has made him a sought-after speaker and brilliant teacher of Truth.

Rev. Nancy Berggren, author of *Life is a Game and You Can Play It*

"It takes courage to step into our power, very often that means walking through fear," which is one of many edicts Rev. Dr. Ron Fox challenges us to do. His decades as a minister gives him a depth of experience on how to help others live their best faith-based life.

Readers will find the topics and guidance offered in this book relatable, inspirational, and motivational! "In the most difficult of times we can experience peace, love, wholeness, serenity, and healing." This is one of many motivational pronouncements Rev. Dr. Ron Fox offers readers.

Yolanda Porter, assistant editor Science of Mind magazine (2004 to 2008)

GUIDES FOR DAILY LIVING

Experiencing the Beacon Within

TELL IT LIKE IT COULD BE

Everyday, life gives us an opportunity to live our dreams. We can use our spiritual power to create heaven on earth for ourselves. What we think, believe, and say today is the life we are creating for tomorrow. We must focus on what we wish to experience, because focusing on what we don't want will never manifest what we do want.

Ernest Holmes wrote, "Our belief sets the limit to our demonstration of a principle which Itself is without limit." The only thing that caps our experience of all the good that is available to us is our own belief system. If we believe we will only receive a little, that is what the universe provides, but as our faith and belief expand so does our demonstration.

Releasing old beliefs is not easy. It takes work, hard work to transform ourselves. But the good news is that it can be done. With dedication and persistence, we can release limiting beliefs and see life differently. We are never bound by what has come before and it is never too late to begin. In the Tao it is written, "When I let go of what I am, I become what I might be. When I let go of what I have, I receive what I need." Why not step up and give it a try today?

"The point of power is always in the present moment. You are never stuck." Louise Hay

LIVE FOR TODAY

Our life is unfolding in the present. Yet so often we spend our time worrying about the future or regretting the past. Ernest Holmes teaches us that we are constantly living a new life, and when the old and new do not nicely fit together, the old should be disregarded. He taught that we should stay open at the top because there will always be new revelations of old truths. That doesn't mean we throw out the good that the past has to offer, but we convert it to greater good.

There is a wonderful Zen story about two monks walking on a trail when they come to a fast-moving river. A young woman is standing there weeping because she is afraid to cross it. The older monk picks her up and carries her across, hours later the young monk begins to scold him because he touched a woman which is forbidden in their order. The older monk replies, "I put her down hours ago but you are still carrying her." Think about the times you may have carried an incident from the past into the present. When we do, we create our own prison and see ourselves as victims rather than the powerful beings we are. What issue are you carrying that needs to be left by the river?

"If you worry about what might be, and wonder what might have been, you will ignore what is." Anonymous

LIVING A LIMITLESS LIFE

Great athletes or performers are no different than we are. There is only one difference. They know what they want, and they are willing to go for it no matter how difficult the challenge. As the quote below implies, dreaming is wonderful, but life does not end with a dream. We must be bold and act on our dreams.

Ernest Holmes reminds us that the prodigal son remained prodigal for as long as he chose. When he returned to his Father's house, he was greeted with open arms. When we release limiting thoughts, we too shall experience a new life. As Dr. Holmes writes, "We shall build a new heaven and a new earth, not in some far-off place but here and now."

Recently I saw a poignant quote from the actor Michael Landon who made his transition way too soon, "Somebody should tell us right at the start of our lives that we are dying. Then we might live life to the limit, every minute of every day. Do It! I say, whatever you want to do, do it now." There are only so many tomorrows. No one can live our life for us. Each of us must make the choice to open ourselves to that still small voice and allow Spirit to express through us. To do anything less is to dishonor the gift of life we have been given.

"What you can do, or dream you can, begin it. Boldness has genius, power and magic in it." Goethe.

YOUR LIFE AS A GIFT

Recently I saw a story about Joseph Campbell. He was in a restaurant and saw a family having a dispute because a little boy would not eat his vegetables. His mother, wanting to end the conflict, told him it was okay not to eat them. His dad exploded saying, "He can't do what he wants in life. I'm forty years old and I've never done anything I wanted in my whole life." Isn't that sad? The dad was totally unaware that he was free to live his life however he chose.

Terry Cole Whittaker wrote, "We have the power to be what we want to be, do what we want to do, and have what we want to have. It all depends on our conscious choices." We were not born to suffer. We were born to have wonderful lives. This is our time to use the gifts we were given so why not step out and shine?

Eric Butterworth believed that the most wide-spread disease of our time is, "I can't itis." We learn it very early from our elders. But the truth is the only thing that limits us is our thoughts. We have the power to choose. We choose and mind creates. So, will you choose thoughts that keep you in a prison of lack and victimhood, or thoughts that liberate you and take your life to places you have dreamed about? It's your pick.

"I always wanted to be somebody, but now I see I should have been more specific." Lily Tomlin

YOU ARE THE ONE

Ernest Holmes writes that the hardest thing we have to do is learn to trust the universe. We like to dabble, pray, and pull it back to see if it's taking hold. The reality is what we need to do is know we are one with the only power that is. The great example for us is Jesus. He had no question that Spirit responded to him the way he wished it to. It responded because he never doubted. And the great message for us is when we can develop a belief that the Universe will respond to us in kind.

Our mind is such a powerful tool. I read recently about a terminal patient who was given a drug that seemed to cure him over night. He then heard it was ineffective and relapsed. His doctor told him the report was false and he again recovered, only to read once again it was a hoax. Two days later he made his transition. When we change how we think we take ourselves to a new place of consciousness and we manifest to the level of that consciousness.

Many of us are taught that living our dreams is not realistic, so we live in our small world of safety. We stay blissfully in our comfort zone living a life that is less than we could enjoy if we were willing to step into our power. There is no better time than now to step up and say yes to the life you are seeking. It's waiting for you just around the corner.

"Follow your heart and intuition, they somehow already know what you truly want to become." Steve Jobs

STAYING CENTERED IN DIFFICULT TIMES

We all go through difficult times, sometimes it seems like the pain will never end. Yet, if we have faith and keep to our spiritual practice, we will move through any situation usually stronger and wiser than before. The truth is we can get through what we think we can't. We don't give our self enough credit for what we can do.

When we face great challenges, we are always at choice. We can let them drag us down and see ourselves as victims, or we can deal with the pain and move to a new place of being. There are those among us that have suffered great tragedies, but they were able to put their lives back together by continuing to believe in a power greater than they are. C. S. Lewis reminds us, "Getting over a painful experience is much like crossing monkey bars. You have to let go at some point in order to move forward." When we let go and let God guide, we can surmount any challenge. As Ernest Holmes reminds us, "With God all things are possible."

Everything in life will change. Over and over we read in the Bible, "It came to pass. Our problem is we want to hold on for dear life. Sometimes we move kicking and screaming from one situation to another. The truth is we cannot control life so we must move to a place of trust and peace as we encounter life's verities. Thich Nhat Hanh wrote, "We think that impermanence makes us suffer. It is not impermanence that makes us suffer. What makes us suffer is wanting things to be permanent when they are not."

"I am not what happened to me. I am what I choose to become." Carl Gustav

NO QUICK FIX

Recently, I saw a study on the religious attitudes of baby boomers. As they matured, they learned spirituality must be a continual practice not a quick fix. For most of us change happens incrementally. We can't overcome years of conditioning with one prayer or workshop. We must be willing to do the hard work to change old beliefs, habits, patterns, and choices. When we are willing to do that our life unfolds joyfully and peacefully. As my late friend Reverend Tom Costa used to say, "Yea, though I walk through the valley of the shadow of death, I don't have to stop and build a condo there."

I read a story by a lady named Anne Fullerton about her dad. He was 93 and had had a very successful career. Now he was legally blind and deaf. After one particularly difficult day she met him at the ferry and before she could console him he said, "You know I'm learning to love what is." How wise. We all need to learn to love our life as it is unfolding. When we remember that beyond all appearances Spirit is with us in the middle of every situation, perhaps we can gain some comfort from that. Every day is a blessing and a gift. When we remember that in good times and the not so good times, we walk life's path much more easily.

"The unfolding of the human heart is artful and mysterious."
Jack Kornfield

THE MYTH OF PERFECTION

How often do we measure our self-worth by what others think of us? That is a very stressful way to live. We are constantly trying to live up to someone else's view of a perfect life, and when we don't, we judge our self as being inadequate. We all make mistakes. We all have moments when we aren't at our best but that's because we are human. It has nothing to do with our innate goodness or worthiness.

Sometimes our worst moments can be a gift that leads us to our best moments. Roger Bannister was the first person to run a mile in less than four minutes. What is not as well known is the year before he was the favorite to win the Olympics, but he did not. Because of that he decided to keep running. Had he won the Olympics, he would have retired from racing and gone to medical school. So, an apparent failure led to his greatest success.

The quote below from Michael Bernard Beckwith is so comforting to me. No matter what we do our divinity is never touched. We are still the perfect spiritual beings we were created to be. If we are willing to do our spiritual work, we can make the outer like the inner. In her book, *Guidance From the Darkness*, Reverend Mary Murray Shelton recounts a heartwarming story about her son Luke. Luke was running cross country, and she went to watch. He came in last. As she went to console him, Luke was all excited, "Mom I beat my personal best by a whole second" he said. It's all a matter of perspective.

"Self-acceptance which is independent of the praise from the outside world accelerates our potential for growth because it nurtures us from within." Michael Bernard Beckwith

WHAT DO YOU EXPECT?

The quality of our life depends on the quality of our thoughts. What we expect from life is what we will manifest. Circumstances don't create our life we do. So, if we want our outer world to improve, we need to begin working on our inner world first. As we say in Religious Science, a new cause will produce a new effect. Brian Tracy asks, "What's better than positive thinking?" He answers, "Positive knowing," where you know with certainty you can achieve something, and you expect the universe to back you.

Years ago, a couple in the center I was ministering to came and asked me what the church needed. It seems every six to eight weeks they went to Loughlin to gamble and bought the center something with their winnings. I suggested a microwave and the next week we had one. One time we received a TV set and lots of cash. I can't say they always won but in the time I knew them, they never lost. They had no doubt that they would be successful and they were. One day when we were talking about their success at gambling, they laughed and said, "You're the teacher we are just practicing what you taught us. So, what if it's in a casino, God is there too."

"If it's going to be, it's up to me." Robert Shuller

THE OPEN DOOR

Emmet Fox wrote about a poor painter who couldn't even afford a canvas. One day he sees an old painting for sale and purchases it. As he begins to clear off the canvas so he can paint on it he sees another picture underneath. It turns out to be from one of the masters and he sells it, and is poor no more. You and I may often look like we are damaged and imperfect on the surface. Our spiritual work is to erase these false images, so our true beauty can shine through.

Too often we allow the world's opinions and beliefs to define us. We begin to believe in our limitations. We can move beyond these ideas. Ernest Holmes reminds us, "To learn how to think is to learn how to live." As we learn the truth about who we really are, we can rise above limiting thoughts and live as the divine emanations we are.

Michelangelo wrote, "The greater danger for most of us lies not in setting our aim too high and falling short; but in setting our aim too low, and achieving our mark." We are all capable of achieving great things. There is no limit to what we can do when we allow Spirit to guide our lives. God is in all of us. We are inseparable. As we come to understand this and open the door to allow Spirit to express in all we do, our life blossoms like a beautiful flower.

"The eye, through which I see God, is the same eye through which God sees me. My eye and God's eye are one eye, one seeing, one knowing, one love." Meister Eckhart

COUNTING OUR BLESSINGS

Eric Butterworth teaches us that thanksgiving is not just a reactionary emotion it is a causative energy. God doesn't care if we give thanks, but it does make a difference to us. It is a state of consciousness that keeps us in tune with the divine flow. It's easy to get caught up in the idea that life isn't going right, or we can see life as a gift even in the tough times.

Rabbi Baruch Spinoza was an early advocate of developing a gratitude practice. He said every day for a month you should ask yourself three questions: "Who or what inspired me today? What brought me happiness today? What brought me comfort and deep peace today?" He said if we did this it would help us find more joy and meaning in our life and lead to inner transformation. When we focus on what is positive and affirming in our life, we attract more of that into our everyday circumstances.

So, how can we begin a gratitude practice? Write someone a thank you note or call them to offer appreciation for something they did for you. Begin a gratitude list. Before you go to sleep at night write down five things you are grateful for that day. At the end of the week you will have 35 things to be grateful for. Write affirmations. I just read about someone who carries a gratitude rock with them. Every time they touch it they silently say thank you. Whatever you do, remember every day to give thanks for the people and wonders that surround you. They are all a blessing.

"Everything that happens to us in life does so to make us more holy." Scott Peck

THE BEAUTY OF A NEW DAY

At the grave of Lazarus, Jesus instructs his friends to remove the stone. It's important to note Jesus did not ask God to remove the stone, because God cannot. We need to remove it. If there are barriers that are preventing us from living life fully, we need to remove them. You and I have the power to change our lives, whenever we decide to.

Rumi tells us in the quote below what we seek is seeking us. What is that? For me it's a closer walk with God. So, what stops me? I get caught up in my life. Things, like my job, my family, my fears get in my way and I forget I am a child of God.

Tony Robbins has a list of 10 empowering beliefs, number 10 is, "Every day above ground is a great day." When we remember that we can focus on the fact our life is a gift, we should treat it as such. We can give thanks every day for our life and move beyond the petty annoyances of the dust and grit that get in our way. We can also remember that the power that created all that is awaits our recognition to step forth to guide us to a more satisfying and successful life.

"What you are seeking is also seeking you." Rumi

LIFE GOES ON

Life is fragile. We never know when our time on this planet will be over. Our teaching offers us hope of more to come after our time here is complete. Ernest Holmes taught that we are immortal, we will continue on after the experience of physical death. He wrote, "We need fear nothing in the Universe. We need not be afraid of God. We may be certain that all will be at the final goal, and no one will be missing."

When he was seventeen Steve Jobs read, "If you live each day as if it could be your last, someday you will be right." For me that is a call to use my time here well. Each day is a gift. Many of us live limited fearful lives, when we were put here to do wondrous things with our time. Dr. Holmes writes that there is a voice that calls us to, "Arise and come forth." A voice that urges us to live a full and expansive life, where there are no limits other than the ones we choose to believe in.

In 2011, Nobel Laurite Elie Wiesel almost died. He later wrote that what he learned from that experience was that every day is a new beginning, every handshake a promise. He continued, "If life is not a celebration why remember it? If life is not an offering to the other what are we doing on this earth?" Ask yourself how do I want to be remembered, and then live into that image.

"Everyone has got to die, but I have always believed an exception would be made in my case." William Saroyan

THIS IS WHAT I KNOW

Staying centered in difficult times is not easy. A while back a friend of ours was very sick, in the depth of her pain she asked us, "Where is God?" We spent time with her listening and sharing what we hoped would be comforting thoughts. She began to meditate and use guided meditations. A short while later she emailed us, she knew there was only God and her. As we do our spiritual work, we see God everywhere.

The Buddhist teacher, Jack Kornfield, says one of the most difficult things about hard times is we think we are alone, but we aren't. He related a time when he was leading a workshop with Pema Chodrin with about 3,000 people in attendance. Someone stood up and related her great pain at losing her partner to suicide a few weeks prior. Jack asked everyone in the audience who had ever lost a loved one to suicide to stand. About two hundred people rose.

No matter what appearances seem to be, Spirit is always with us. We are never alone. Jesus taught that if a friend came to us at midnight to ask for bread we would not turn him away. He said, "Ask and it shall be given to you, seek and you shall find, knock and it shall be opened unto you." Spirit never refuses anyone. So next time you are hurting, remember that as you turn within to seek peace and healing, before you even ask your prayer is being answered.

"A man is the product of his thoughts. What he thinks he becomes." Mohandas K. Gandhi

STEPPING INTO THE UNKNOWN

I read that in olden times, armies would burn the bridges they crossed when the moved into enemy territory. There was no turning back. You and I can't cling to the old and enjoy the new at the same time. We can't cling to what was if we want to step into the yet to be. In the song, *"Keeping the Faith"* Billy Joel has a lyric that goes, "You know the good ole days weren't always good, And tomorrow ain't as bad as it seems."

It always comforts me to remember that, "Spirit isn't bound by precedent." Just because the past didn't live up to my expectations does not mean I am doomed to repeat it. In fact, sometimes pain can be our greatest teacher. Ernest Holmes reminds us, "The possibilities of the Law are infinite, and our possibilities of using it are limitless." So, if I am willing to embrace new ways of thinking and being, I can create a whole new life for myself. I decide what life will show me. What I envision for myself I can manifest. Perhaps this unknown author put it best, "When we walk to the edge of all the light we have, and take the step into the darkness of the unknown; we must believe that one of two things will happen, there will be something solid for us to stand on, or we will be taught to fly."

"Being friends with the unknown, with the sure knowledge that we don't know how things will turn out, means learning to take refuge in the moment-by-moment of what is, rather than a belief in what may or may not come to be."
Joan Borysenko

STANDING IN YOUR TRUTH

Ernest Holmes tells us Jesus did not have special powers that others did not possess. He was able to do what he did because he believed in what he taught. He so completely lived his teachings that he was able to demonstrate them. You and I can demonstrate what we teach and believe too. We begin by putting our complete trust in Spirit. It is written in the Tao Te Ching, "When I let go of what I am, I become what I might be. When I let go of what I have, I receive what I need."

We live in a world where fear seems to be everywhere. If we can't overcome our fears, we will never be able to live the life we desire. We need to be willing to move beyond our comfort zone. And, trust in Spirit, as Andre Gide reminds us, "Man cannot discover new oceans, unless he has the courage to lose sight of the land."

Recently, I read a story about a monk that built a brick wall. When the wall was completed, he realized two bricks were at an angle and he was embarrassed. When he showed it to someone, they remarked that the wall was beautiful. The monk asked, "Can't you see the two that are at an angle?" The man replied, "Yes but I also see the 998 that aren't." Sometimes we are way too hard on ourselves; we see only where we have not lived up to our standards. We need to move beyond what the world tells us and know we are God expressing, instead of being harsh with ourselves. Remember, there are no mistakes only opportunities to grow and learn.

"You are what you repeatedly do. Excellence is not an event, it is a habit." Aristotle

WALKING THROUGH FEAR

We all have fears, it's a normal part of life. But, if we allow our fears to prevent us from living a full life, we lose out on much of the joy and excitement of living. Howard Falco in his book, *I AM*, writes, "Your story will be your story until it was your story." When we learn to move beyond fear we can change our story from one of limitation to one of expansive and creative living. We are the authors, so we get to decide when a re-write is necessary.

Nelson Mandela wrote, "I learned that courage was not the absence of fear, but the triumph over it. The brave man is not he who does not feel afraid, but he who conquers that fear." How can we conquer fear? When we develop a spiritual practice, we learn to trust in Spirit and develop a faith that allows us to put fear in our rear-view mirror. As we realize we are surrounded and indwelled by a loving and powerful Presence that is willing to work with and through us, we come to see how blessed we are.

"When you become comfortable with uncertainty, infinite possibilities open up in your life." Eckhart Tolle

Reconciliation:

Moving Past the Hurt

Jesus gave us two great commandments: love God and love our fellow man. Ernest Holmes tells us that there is a complete unity with life. Loving God is not enough because that excludes our fellow man. He wrote, "The alter of faith is approached through peace and goodwill toward all."

Immacule Illibiaza, lost her mother, father and brother in the war in Rwanda. Years later she was brought to a prison to meet the man who was the leader of the group that killed her family. She reached out and told him that she forgave him. The warden asked her why and her reply was, "Forgiveness is all I have to offer." That is what Jesus meant when he said we must forgive 70 x 7. We need to move beyond our hurts and allow God to bring us healing.

Years ago, I attended a lecture by a woman who spent years in a German concentration camp and lost her entire family. After the lecture I went to ask her a question. Before I could complete my question, she interrupted me and said, "You want to know if I have forgiven them." I said yes, and she replied, "Of course I did. If not, hate would have consumed me and I could not let that happen." When we forgive our enemies, we realize we have no enemies. What a peaceful place to be.

"No matter what is happening in the world of appearances, beyond the veil of illusion there is love and only love."
Marianne Williamson

THE POWER OF CHOICE

Jesus said, "You will know the truth and the truth shall set you free." As we move forward with our life it is not enough to read about the truth or listen to lectures about the truth, we must know the truth. When we are facing adversity, we must have already done our work, so our response comes from a place of faith. We must know that the divine presence is with us always and there is nothing we cannot successfully overcome.

A minister of mine told a story about the choices we make in life. A policeman was called to the scene of a burglary, and promptly arrested the culprit, who turned out to be his brother. Sometime later a reporter interviewed both men. The policeman said, "My father was an alcoholic how else could I turn out?" His brother told the reporter, "My father was an abusive drunk how else could I turn out?" The same circumstances two different results. We choose what we see from life. We must take responsibility for our actions, blaming only gives our power away and keeps us in the same predicaments. When we are willing to take responsibility for our life, we can begin to make choices that bring us healing and help us live the life of our choice, rather than being stuck in a never ending cycle of blame, anger and victimhood.

"It's only a thought and a thought can be changed."
Louise Hay

THE HUMBLE SERVANT

The quote below by Wayne Muller touches me. Life's hurts can make us bitter or remind us we are here to grow. In our humanness we all hurt at times and we all can choose our response. Jesus had the ability to look beyond appearances and see God everywhere. You and I can learn to do that too.

In the Gospel of Luke, Jesus is asked, "Who is my neighbor?" His response is to tell the parable of the good Samaritan, a mixed-race person who saves the life of a Jew that had been mugged, when others had passed by him. The message is clear, everyone is our neighbor, and everyone is worthy of love and respect. As Ernest Holmes wrote, "Who finds God in man, will also find man in God."

Rabbi Harold Kushner says when people ask him, "Where is God?" His response is, "A better question is when is God?" Finding God is not being in the right place but rather doing the right thing. We make room for God when we do the things that make us truly human. "When we get over being stuck on ourselves, we make room for God."

"To learn humility is to honor that your hurt and mine are one, that we share the gentle communion of being human."
Wayne Muller

CHOOSING PEACE

There is a fable that describes a king who offered a prize for the person who could paint the best picture of peace. There were two finalists. One drew a picture of peaceful mountains, fluffy clouds, and a calm lake. The other drew a picture of an angry sky, lightening, and a rushing waterfall. Behind the waterfall was a tiny bush growing from a crack in a rock, there sat a mother bird in her nest in perfect calm. The king chose the second picture, for reasons the anonymous author described, "Peace doesn't mean to be in a place where there is no noise, trouble or hard work. It means to be in the midst of these things and still be calm in your heart."

Thich Nhat Hanh wrote about how people responded to the stress of crowded refugee boats when they encountered storms or pirates. He said, "If everyone panicked the boat would capsize. If only one person remained calm and centered in God that was enough to save everyone." What a wonderful example of how powerful our faith can be, not only do we affect our own life but the lives of everyone around us. When we choose peace, we experience God. No matter what appearances seem to be, deep within we are calm and serene, because we know all is well, and life is unfolding just as it should.

"Every day brings a choice: to practice stress or to practice peace." Joan Borysenko

WE ARE MORE THAN OUR DIFFERENCES

We live in a time when we seem to define ourselves more by our differences than by what we have in common. How do we rise above the daily events of life? Ernest Holmes said we must realize that the God in us meets the God in everyone else. We are one with Spirit and each other. Our job is to allow Spirit to flow throw us so we can receive divine guidance and direction.

In Matthew 7:3 Jesus asks, "Why do you see the pole in your brother's eye, and not the beam in your own eye?" It is so easy to see faults in someone else and overlook our own shortcomings. Our perception gets distorted and we feel superior. Yet in God's eyes we are all precious.

In his book, *The Power of Kindness*, Piero Ferrucci, writes there are two world views. We can distance ourselves by suspicion, or we can draw nearer to people knowing we are linked to one another. One is a very pessimistic view, the other is more optimistic. In our life, trust and kindness are linked. Kindness brings us closer to people. As Nelsa Curbelo writes, "Everything in society tells us to distrust others. I think it's the other way around. We need to profoundly trust in those around us, in their potential and in who they are. When we do, our love is returned tenfold."

"Seek not to change the world, but to change your mind about the world." A Course in Miracles

THE GIFTS OF COMMUNITY

Rachel Remen recounts a story that speaks to how important connection is for all of us. Every month a homeless woman saw the head of a family medicine clinic. He always treated her with respect and dignity. After a while he found out she was coming to the clinic on days he was not there. She never went into his room, but she put her foot in and took it out, again and again. Then she would leave. Remen wrote, "The places in which we are seen and heard are holy places. They remind us of our value as human beings. They give us the strength to go on."

It is not always easy to accept people on their terms. We open our hearts to those we like and those we do not like. We broaden our thinking and accept that we are all doing the best we can as children of God. We must come together and see our oneness rather than how we are different.

Ananda, a close friend of the Buddha, met a woman at a well. He asked her for a drink and she refused because she was an untouchable and would contaminate him. He responded, "I ask not for caste but for water." This simple act of kindness transformed her life. She met the Buddha who advised her, "Let the actions of your life shine like the jewels of royalty." That seems like wonderful advice for all of us.

"The only devils in the world are the ones running around in our own hearts. This is where the battle must be fought."
Mohandas K. Gandhi

BEING REAL

Being real means being true to ourselves, listening to our inner voice and following it. It means living our ideals rather than just talking about them. Ernest Holmes wrote, "We must learn to live by inspiration. That means we should let the spiritual depths of our being flow through our conversation and into our acts." Notice he speaks about our acts. Speaking isn't enough, we must live our principles. It's not always easy to do especially if friends and family are not in agreement with us. Being true to our self is essential to living a happy and centered life.

The late Reverend Florence Phillips wrote that three of the most powerful words in our language are, "Just do it." It's easy to sit and let life pass us by, especially if we are frozen with fear. Taking action is a lesson we need to learn over and over again. As we step into our power we gain more confidence in our self, and it's never too late to start believing in yourself.

There is an old Hasidic tale about a rabbi named Zusya. He was getting on in years and one of his students asked him what he feared most about dying. His response was, "I am afraid of what they will ask me when I get to heaven." His student responded, "What do you think they will ask you?" They will ask me, "Zusya why were you not Zusya?" In other words, why were you not true to who you are? Why did you live someone else's truth and not your own? If we walk our talk, it's a question we will never have to answer.

"If you bring forth what is within you it will save you. If you do not bring forth what is within you, it will kill you."
The Gospel of Thomas

A Time for Renewal

Life is not static, it moves forward. Renewal is a deep process. In an article, Dr. David Alexander asks us to imagine waking up every day and all the gifts you ever wanted are waiting for you. Well they are. They are the gifts Spirit brings to us, and they are ours for the taking. All we need to do is create a space to accept them. As we invite Spirit into our lives in a bigger way we are renewed and invigorated.

Ernest Holmes tells us that our true nature is divine, and all of us are a center for activity of the consciousness of God. So, if God is acting in and through us all the time there is nothing we can experience that we cannot handle. No matter what life is showing us we have the greatest power in the universe working with us. Any moment can be a time of renewal for us. We get to choose our response to any external stimulus and when we act with the consciousness of God as our guide we can never go wrong.

What if today you made the decision to release the status quo and to really live your dreams? You can do that. You don't have to wait for some holiday to make a resolution; any day can be a day of renewal. You can decide right now to say yes to Spirit and begin to live a fuller more joyful life. It's all up to you. What are you waiting for?

"Within a holy relationship one never looks for what one can get, but only what one can joyfully share." Christine Smith

BACK TO BASICS

I love our philosophy. It is so freeing. Ernest Holmes' teaching is empowering, we learn that there are no victims; my life is in my hands to create as I choose. We are free to turn within and work with Spirit, or to choose to go it alone. And whichever way we choose, a loving Creator awaits our recognition, and will answer our every prayer.

There is a fable about a great statue of the Buddha which is made of pure gold. It resides in a monastery. One day the monks hear that an army is coming so they cover the statue with mud, stones and mortar. The army does not discover it. Many years later a piece of the concrete chips off and the Golden Buddha was discovered. The lesson is that no matter what our appearances are within us there is a loving and wise presence that is available to us. We can cover it up, but we can never destroy it. That is what Meister Eckhart is saying in the quote below, to achieve spiritual transformation we need not add anything, we must just remove the dirt and grime of life.

Ernest Holmes teaches that we are surrounded by infinite possibility that wishes to express through us. As we open to it, it becomes the Law of our Life. Alan Cohen puts it beautifully, "Peace must come to those who ask for it. Strength must be given to those who claim it. And love must bring healing to all who open to receive it. The time of awakening is at hand."

"Spiritual transformation is a process of elimination not addition." Meister Eckhart

SPIRITUAL RESILIENCE

So often we see people in pain, the ravages of war, and all sorts of injustice. It's often difficult not to react in kind, yet we know we must not. In times like this we must listen to our inner voice and choose love and peace. Ernest Holmes reminds us, "The man who has arrived will realize that he has done so in the midst of an outer confusion. He will be the one who has gone into the silence for strength." No matter what we see in life we are never alone. A great and loving power is always with us.

We are all going to face hardships in life, that is part of living, but we get to choose how we will respond. Will we turn bitter? Or will we be resilient and turn within for guidance? King Soloman was often depressed and uncertain. He had a dream that a ring existed that would bring him peace. He called some of his followers together and ordered them to find it. It took a while but when they did the ring was presented to him and it simply read, "This too shall pass." Everything is impermanent.

When we go through tough times, we gain strength and courage. We realize that we have a power that we might never have experienced before. So, the next time we face adversity we know we can meet it and move through it. It might help to remember these words from *A Course in Miracles*, "Trials are but lessons that you failed to learn presented once again."

"Remember strength based in force is a strength people fear. Strength based in love is a strength people crave."
Kent Nerburn

BEGINNING ANEW

Did you ever wonder what our life and the world would be like if we really took to heart the teachings of the world's spiritual masters? Piero Ferrucci writes on kindness. He had a friend who asked her dad, "What is the most important thing in life?" Her dad responded, "To forgive." Here was a man whose entire first family was killed in the holocaust. We can't imagine the horror he endured yet he can forgive and declare it is the most important value in life.

Tolstoy has a story about a poor shoemaker who hears the voice of Christ in a dream, "Today I will come to you." He goes to work and throughout the day helps many people. At the end of the day he goes home and thinks the dream did not come true since he did not see Christ. Again, the voice comes and reminds him of the people helped all day. Christ says, "I was with each of them and with you all day." Ernest Holmes wrote, "It is not enough to say there is one life and that life is God." We must complete the statement by saying "and that life is my life now." When we do, we make God's life our life.

What is most important in life are the moments we reach out and touch one another. When we show our caring for one another and let another know they are not alone. As Mother Teresa said, "In this life we cannot do great things, we can only do small things with great love."

"Nothing is precious except that part of you which is in other people, and that part of others which is in you. Up there, on high, everything is one." Pierre Teilhard de Chardin

HEALING POWER

We were not created to suffer. Ernest Holmes tells us, "The possibility of healing disease, changing our environment, attracting friends, and demonstrating supply, rests entirely on the theory that we are surrounded by an infinite mind which reacts to our thought." The only limitation on this infinite mind is the one we place there.

In *The Principles of Healing*, H. B. Jeffrey, the one who does the best healing is the one who sees nothing to be done, because he sees only God. When we turn within and totally accept our oneness with Spirit, we become healers. Jeffrey tells us like Paul, we can say, "I know whom I have believed."

There are so many examples of people being cured of diseases when they took placebos, which are nothing more than sugar pills, but they believed the pills were powerful. I have even read about people who underwent operations that were actually shams but the patients did not know this and they had the same cure rate as those who underwent the actual operation. Our minds are powerful tools.

When we think the same thoughts, we will get the same results. When we change our beliefs, we can change the demonstrations we see. By changing how we think we can change our brain and that will lead to changes in our body. Joe Dispenza says, "We become our own placebo."

"When we change our thoughts, behaviors and beliefs, we can change our biology. We are masters of our lives, not the victim of our genes." Bruce Lipton

OPENING TO OUR ABUNDANCE

Eric Butterworth says we are human magnets. We draw to us the things, people and circumstances that match our thinking. Wherever we are in our life is because of where we are in consciousness. Our belief system creates our reality.

Jesus said, "It is done unto you as you believe." Ernest Holmes said what a marvelous thought, no need to coerce or beg; all we need to do is allow this great power to operate through us, and as the quote below states, "We are drawn silently toward it."

In the Bible, Jesus tells a parable about a master who is going away, and he entrusts several of his servants with coins. When he returns, two of the servants have invested wisely while the third buried his coin. The master takes the one coin and gives it to the man with ten, saying, "For to everyone who has more will be given, and he will have abundance, but from him who has not even what he has will be taken away." We know Jesus was not a cruel person so what could he have meant? I believe he is telling us to find the gifts we have and use them wisely, multiply them. Don't hide your gifts. Ask yourself, "What would my life be like if I used all my gifts?"

"The goal should not be to make money or acquire things, but to achieve the consciousness through which the substance will flow forth when and as you need it."
Eric Butterworth

THE HIDDEN BLESSINGS IN OBSTACLES

Pir Vilayat Inayat Khan, a Sufi master, writes that so many of us don't see the spiritual dimensions of life itself. We see them as frustrations. Yet we can find illumination in our everyday activities. Instead of a permanent roadblock, they are what he calls, "Creative catalysts for spiritual evolution." Most of us are aware that butterflies must struggle in the cocoon in order to survive and send fluids to their wings so they may fly. The struggle is necessary for transformation.

Very often when we face an obstacle, we find out how strong we really are. We find that the spiritual work we have been doing is paying off. Recently, I learned a friend was in hospice, so I called her. She had a terrible cough that made talking almost impossible, so I suggested I call back the next day. She responded, "OK, but I may not be here." The next day her cough was better, and we had a long talk. I asked her how the spiritual work she had done for most of her adult life was helping her get through this time. She said it was difficult to express how her faith was supporting her. She said, "My faith in God is so strong I am ready for whatever comes next." Two days later she made her transition.

"Obstacles are necessary for success. Each struggle, each defeat, sharpens your skills and strengths, your courage and your endurance." Og Mandino

ONENESS

There is a power within us that can lead us to happiness and peace. So, all of the knowledge and wisdom we will ever need is always available to us, and you and I get to choose how and if we will use it. We can live as victims or spiritual powerhouses. We can give our power away by blaming other people for our difficulties, or we can take responsibility for any issues in our life and thereby claim our power.

There is a fable about a prince that falls in love with a beautiful maiden who lives in a palace. He knocks on the door and she asks, "Who is It?" He responds, "It is I your prince." She tells him there is only room for one of us here. This scene repeats itself several times until finally the prince responds, "It is thou," and the door opens. The prince had to let go of his separate identity to gain entrance. As we give up our separate identity from Spirit, we experience the power and majesty of a wise and loving creator.

There are times in life when it is easy to feel overwhelmed. It's not easy to remember that Spirit is in every situation we encounter. Having faith requires us to look beyond appearances and to know that Spirit is always with us in the dark times and the light times. We are always one.

"You are never given a wish without also being given the power to make it true. You may have to work for it however."
Richard Bach

UNLOCKING OUR UNLIMITED POTENTIAL

Studies show that people are less afraid of dying than they are of living a life that did not matter. That they might as well have never lived. We all have a gift and in order to feel fulfilled we must develop and use it. When we do, we are not only serving our purpose, we are serving humanity. The great Olympic runner Gail Devers wrote, "Success does not mean you have to be number one… It means you have to give it your all."

Benjamin Zander came from a family of four children. Every night at the dinner table his father would ask each son, "What did you do today?" Benjamin wrote that the question really meant, "What did you achieve today?" He thinks that a better question would be, "How will you be a contribution today?" This question speaks to how we can serve best, how we are using our gifts to help our fellow humans. What are you doing to unlock your potential? What would happen if instead of striving to be best and to compete, we simply asked the question, "how can I serve?"

"When I stand before God at the end of my life, I would hope I would not have a single bit of talent left, and I could say, 'I used everything you gave me'." Erma Bombeck

ACCEPTING WHAT IS

I read recently that when hot air balloons are being filled the wind can buffet them so much that it seems like the ropes they are tethered to will not be able to hold them. However, once it ascends everything becomes quiet. The balloon is riding with the currents, there is no resistance. The same is true for us when we resist what life is showing us, we experience pain and stress. When we deny what is, we suffer. We do not have to like it, but we do have to acknowledge it.

Eckhart Tolle reminds us that surrender is not a negative concept. It is not giving up; it is simply accepting the present moment unconditionally and without reservation. He writes, "It is letting go of resistance to what is." The beauty of doing this is that then we can begin to work at changing the condition. If we are in denial, we can't move past it.

Accepting what is, is not always easy. However, even in times of distress we can look for deeper meaning in what is occurring. We can ask ourselves what is the lesson in this? Ernest Holmes tells us to never become discouraged and to keep doing our work. Spirit always responds. After all, as Byron Katie writes, "When you argue with reality you lose, but only 100% of the time."

"We cannot change anything until we accept it." Carl Jung

Forgiveness

Years ago, my wife and I took our youngest son to the Los Angeles Holocaust Museum. It was a solemn day. One of the activities we experienced was a lecture by a survivor of one of Hitler's concentration camps. After the lecture I asked her if she could ever forgive those who abused her and murdered most of her family. She replied, "Of course I forgive them. Otherwise the hate would have eaten me up." To me that speaks to how indestructible our human spirit is, no matter how unspeakable an experience we may have encountered we can choose to move on and forgive those who caused us such pain.

Forgiveness allows us to move on with our life. We release the burdens of anger, pain, and despair and move forward enjoying what life has to offer. Gerald Jampolsky defines forgiveness as, "letting go of all hope for a better past."

Piero Ferrucci compares not forgiving with a city whose traffic is completely congested. The roads are blocked, cars can't move, and garbage can't be collected, as it rots on the side of the road. No one is enjoying life at all. That's what not forgiving is like, rancor generating new rancor blocking vital energy and poisoning life. Forgiving is not for the perpetrator it's for the victim. It frees us from living in the past and as Louis B. Smedes reminds us, we discover we were the prisoner trapped in our own unwillingness to forgive. A heavy burden is released and we feel so much lighter.

"To forgive is to set a prisoner free, and to discover that the prisoner was you." Louis B. Smedes

COURTING THE PRESENCE

In the book *"I Am"* Howard Falco writes, "The greatest message of the universe is, "You matter." He goes on to write, "you are not who you think you are, but always so much more." This is true because we are one with the Divine. Wherever we are and whatever is taking place in our lives we are united with the power that created all that is. When we believe that, we know we do matter.

Ernest Holmes tells us we are spiritual beings right now, as immortal as we ever will be. We are living in God right now and the nature of God is flowing through us right now. So, when we seek guidance or comfort from what life is showing us, we don't need to search or look anywhere but right where we are standing. We are never alone, Spirit is always with us. I find that to be a very comforting thought.

Eric Butterworth tells us, "The activity of God is always seeking to heal you, to bless you, to fill your vessels with good. When you get yourself out of the way, the divine flow does its perfect work." So, when we are willing to put our egos aside and rely on the power within to bring Its loving and healing energy to us, we experience the wonder of Spirit working in our life. We don't need to force anything, just relax and allow God to show you the way to peace, wholeness, love and all the other wonders of life in Spirit. Isn't it worth a try next time life hurts? After all, all you have to lose is pain and fear; that sounds like a really good deal to me. How about you?

"The eye, with which I see God, is the same eye with which God sees me." Meister Eckhart

LIVING A LEGACY

We all want to be remembered for what we have contributed to the lives of those around us after we are gone. That is what a legacy is all about. Most of us aren't going to change the world but we can have an impact on the people in our life. As Mother Teresa reminds us, "In this life we cannot do great things. We can only do small things with great love." And in the end isn't that enough?

In our philosophy we teach that we are all unique. We are not here by accident, and we each have a gift to give. If we don't give that gift no one else can so it is lost forever. We give our gift because when we do, we are living the life we were meant to express, not because of what we may receive in return. Recently I read a story about a woman who went through many challenges in her life. Through it all her father was by her side. Here is what she wrote, "When you strip everything away, all the lipstick, and nail polish, what you're left with is your true self, and that my Dad showed me was something to celebrate." That is a legacy.

Here is an interesting exercise I read about that you may want to try. Imagine it's your 80th birthday; all your friends are there and one by one they get up to toast you. What would you like them to say? That is what you want your life to stand for. If you're happy with what you are imagining great, if not it's never too late to make some changes.

"I want the world to be better because I was here. I want my life, my work, my family to mean something. And if you are not making someone else's life better then you are wasting your time." Will Smith

THE CHALLENGE OF FAITH

I don't believe that faith is something we get. It's having moments when we can say, "I'm getting it." It's a growth process. The step Dr. King refers to in the quote below doesn't have to be a big one; we can begin with small steps and grow. Each time we feel the Presence working in our lives we increase our trust, and before long fear and doubt begin to melt away.

I know that sometimes life can be very scary. We lose a loved one, or a job, or a relationship, and we feel all alone. Appearances can overwhelm us. In these times we need to remember that even on the darkest days, the sun is still shining even though the clouds are hiding it. God is always God and we are never left alone to fend for ourselves. Spirit is always right with us. Jesus reminds us we need to approach Spirit with the faith of a little child. When we approach Spirit, we are never refused. We always get an answer.

This is a Native American prayer I saw recently: "Creator, whatever it is you want me to do today, that is what I want to do. Whatever it is you want me to say today, creator, that is what I want to say. Wherever it is you want me to go today, creator that is where I want to go." What great faith. It is a wonderful example of, "Your will be done." The person who wrote it is telling us he knows wherever he is and whatever he is doing he will be safe. Spirit will be with him. What an example for all of us.

"Faith is taking the first step even when you don't see the whole staircase." Martin Luther King Jr.

WHY DO WE SUFFER?

One of the greatest gifts we have is free choice. It can also cause us great pain. Why you might ask? Having free will implies we have more than one choice. So in our humanness, we can make choices that create pain and suffering to us and those around us. Dr. Holmes wrote, "We must expect to experience the logical result of our thought and acts, be it good or what we call evil."

In our life there will be setbacks and disappointments. They can teach us lessons. When life hurts, we can ask, "What is the lesson in this event?" "How can I grow from it?"

My wife and I just completed facilitating a Foundations class. After we pray in, we begin each class with the following question, "How did God show up in your life this week?" Here is one man's story. He noticed one of his tires was low on air. The next morning, he went to his garage to fill it up and it exploded. He then filled up the spare which was also low but drivable. He bought four new tires, drove a block and his car made a funny sound so he returned to the mechanic. His alternator was broken; he never would have made it home. He saw God in his life because the flat occurred in his garage where he was able to repair it. His car problem happened one block from the mechanic. Where some might have seen only problems, he looked deeper and saw Spirit acting in his life. Lessons abound if we are willing to look beyond what shows up on the surface of our life.

"The wound is the place where the light enters you." Rumi

BEING RECEPTIVE

No matter where we are or what we are encountering, Spirit is always with us. Our task is to be open to recognize that this is so. We must live with an open and receptive heart. Wayne Dyer asked the question, "How do we trust a source we can't see or touch?" His answer was we can tell our self that something is responsible for creating all that we see with our senses and we can choose to trust it from now on.

When I teach a class each week, I ask the students, "How did God show up in your life this week?" The answers are always fascinating. When we look for Spirit, we find it in the most surprising places. I live on a beautiful river. When I write I sit on our back porch. Periodically, I pause and look out at the scene unfolding before me, sometimes I see boats, or dolphins, or manatees, or just a panoramic view of the water. All of it is God in all its beauty.

In the Bible we see countless stories of how faith has healed. A woman believes if she can only touch the hem of Jesus' robe she will be healed. She does and Jesus tells her that her faith has made her whole. Faith is acting even when there is no light. Joseph Campbell tells of a bit of advice given to a young Native American at the time of his initiation, "As you go the way of life, you will see a great chasm. Jump. It is not as wide as you think." As we go the way of life, we will face times where life hurts. Have faith you are not alone. The creator of all is right there with you.

"Have a mind that is open to everything and attached to nothing." Tilopa

WE ARE ONE

A while back I wrote a story about my daughter and her pet pig Wilbur. They love one another, she feeds him, kisses him, and they shower each other with love. Most other people see a rather ugly and foul tempered animal and Wilbur greets them with growls when they go near him. The lesson here is she is willing to go beyond appearances and see the beauty within him and he responds in kind. That works with people too. When we are willing to look beyond surface appearances, we find we have more in common than we ever imagined.

Years ago, I read a story about a nun who told a counselor that she was having a difficult time connecting with her dad. When she went to visit him he wanted to drink beer and watch football. The counselor's advice was, "Next time you go visit leave your habit at home, have a beer with him and see what happens." She followed his advice and reported back that they had a great visit. We put up so many barriers to allowing ourselves to be real with one another. Yet, beyond all our perceived differences we are all one.

We need to embrace our diversity. To not just see our differences but to glory in diversity that Spirit has put forth for our pleasure. Imagine how boring life would be if we all liked the same music or we all looked alike, or prayed alike. There is so much we can learn from one another if we are willing to open ourselves to new experiences. It may help to think about the fact if God loves us and created us just the way we are, how can we do less?

"We work on ourselves then in order to help others. And we help others as a vehicle for working on ourselves."
Paul Gorman and Ram Dass

DISCOVER YOUR SPIRITUAL POWER

Wherever we are and whatever we are doing Spirit is with us. In all we do the entire universe backs us. Many of us believe we are powerless because that is what we have been taught but that is not our truth. The truth is we are powerful spiritual beings and when we believe that, we have infinite potential within just waiting to be manifested.

Whenever we encounter a problem in life, we have an inner guide waiting to be accessed. This guide is the same power that created all that is; yet so often we choose to go it alone, in effect saying to Spirit, "I've got this one." I know the times I have said that I usually end up regretting the decision. You and I have a built in GPS system that is activated 24/7 why not use it?

If you believe you have power, you do. If you believe you do not have power, you don't. In the quote below, Ernest Holmes is telling us what we seek is what we receive. In other words, believe you are a person of power and it will find you. So, next time life hurts believe that you and Spirit have no limits. Go within and seek the divine that awaits your call and see what happens. I'm betting the results are going to be amazing.

"The universe you experience is the current sum total of your beliefs about what is possible." Howard Falco

How to See Yourself as You Really Are

Joel Goldsmith writes that every issue of life is determined by consciousness, not external forces. God is here and now. When we follow spiritual principles, we discover the power within and we manifest our dreams, and we have a personal experience of Spirit.

Alan Cohen tells a fable about a young boy named Willow who wants to become a wizard. However, he fails the test by not answering a question correctly. Years later he and the wizard have a conversation and Willow having grown into manhood answers correctly; that he has learned the power is within him. The wizard then tells him, "Then you have become the master." When we realize that our power resides within, we become the master of our life. We don't fall victim to the vicissitudes of circumstances. We claim our power and move beyond any perceived limitations. Orison Swett Marden put it perfectly when he wrote, "Deep within man dwell these slumbering powers; powers that would astonish him… forces that would revolutionize his life if aroused and put into action."

"There are voices all around telling us who we should be, but somewhere amidst these voices is our own."
Rabbi Dov Heller

SELF-MASTERY

Self-mastery is doing the work to be the best we can be. It is a process of becoming. It is not a final destination. It is not always an easy path invariably there will be setbacks and frustrations. Yet these are the avenues from which we can learn and grow. Neville reminds us that rebirth depends on inner work. We can't be reborn without changing from within. We have all we need to create the life we desire. We just need to tap into it.

Rachel Remen tells the story of a cancer patient who has a dream that a woman is building a mountain. She works day and night and just as she completes the task the mountain begins to collapse on itself. At the last second the woman found that she knew how to fly. When she was asked what she thought it meant she replied, "What we imagine is our strength may be very different from what our strength is."

You and I have a spiritual power that lives within us. As we learn to access and depend on it, we find that we are able to create a life of beauty and wonder. Along the way we come to realize that we are on the road to becoming "the best me I can be," that is self-mastery.

"We must want to be the best we are capable of becoming. If we plan to be less, we will be deeply unhappy for the rest of our life." Abraham Maslow

HONORING ALL PEOPLE

None of us would refuse to help another in need if they were a different religion or had a different sexual orientation than we do. We help because we are all one, and we know it is the right thing to do. People who survived the Oklahoma City bombing said what helped them the most was the love people showed them. People saw each other for what they are: human beings. Psychologist Piero Ferrucci says that a sense of belonging is a basic human need. We can ask, "What am I a part of?"

Last week, I read an article about a former white nationalist who has become an activist against hate. He has a daughter who he does not want to grow up with the hate he did. Now he preaches we are all in this together. Our life is about human connection. Hate has no place here. Rumi tells us, "Out beyond ideas of wrong doing and right doing there is a field. I will meet you there." What a beautiful reminder that when we are willing to move beyond judgment we can meet in that field in love and compassion. And if we disagree, we can do so with kindness and caring.

"I, You, She, We, in the garden of mystic lovers, these are not true distinctions." Rumi

TRANSCENDING FEAR

Mark Twain once remarked that, "Courage is not the absence of fear, but the mastery of it." It means when we face a difficult situation, we don't let fear rule us. Rather, we find the inner strength to confront it, we seek our spiritual power. We remember that at every moment of our life Spirit is with us, so we never have to face any crisis alone. We can move within and find guidance and wisdom, that will carry us through any time of pain and doubt.

When people in the last stages of life are asked to talk about what they most regret, they usually reply it is the opportunities they let slip by not anything they did. Regrets are forever, fear is momentary. When you are in a difficult situation ask yourself, "What is the worst thing that could happen?" Usually it's not what your imagination has been running away with.

I am not big on heights. When I was a pre-teen several of us went to an amusement park. One of the most daunting rides was the parachute jump. A voice told me I had to try it. None of my friends wanted to, but when I offered to pay for one of my friends, he came with me. It was scary and exhilarating. When we came down, he laughed and said, "Let's do it again and this time I'll treat." We both learned a great lesson that day; sometimes fear can be a gift. On that day years ago, fear got us in touch with our courage and we had a great time to boot.

"These then are my last words: Be not afraid of life. Believe that life is worth living and your belief will help create the fact." William James

DIFFERENT WORLD VIEWS: WHAT TO DO?

Wayne Dyer wrote, "If you want peace for others you will receive it. If you want others to receive love you will. When you give away what's in your heart you receive it back." Everyone we meet is holy, when we recognize that we are blessed, because when we treat someone as divine we receive the same treatment.

We all want to live happy peaceful lives. When we treat everyone with care and respect, we all have the opportunity the life of our dreams. When we stop caring about one another we may have the fate Pastor Martin Niemoller describes: "When they came for the communists, I remained silent. I was not a communist. When they locked up the Social Democrats, I remained silent. I was not a Social Democrat. When they came for the Trade Unionists, I did not speak out. I was not a Trade Unionist. When they came for the Jews, I remained silent. I wasn't a Jew. When they came for me, there was no one left to speak out." What a wonderful reminder that we all have a stake in each other's life and happiness.

"If we learn to open our hearts, anyone including people who drive us crazy, can be our teachers." Pema Chodrin

LIVING IN INTEGRITY

Many of us have been taught that we must always "fit in", so we often do not live our truth. We don't speak what is on our heart. We must have the courage to be true to who we really are. Ernest Holmes tells us, "If we allow the world's opinion to control our thinking then that will be our demonstration." When we do that we are giving away our power, and we wind up feeling ashamed and powerless. How often we sell ourselves out because we worry about what the neighbors will think.

Recently I saw this quiz online, "Name the last five Miss Americas, the last five world series winners, the last six best academy award winners for best actor or actress. Most of us can't, but we can remember the names of a few teachers, who helped us along our journey, or others who have helped us to become who we were meant to be. The point is, headlines fade but those who mentored us, and respected us for our gifts are the people we value. If we respect them, should we not respect ourselves enough to live our truth and to speak our truth?

One of my favorite quotes is from Rabbi Abraham Joshua Heschel who wrote, "In the eyes of the world I am average. But in my own heart I am of great moment. The challenge I face is how to actualize, how to concretize the quiet eminence of my own being." We all have the potential to touch the lives of those we are in contact with, to do that we must be willing to step into our truth and speak what we believe. So, the next time you face a situation where you have the opportunity to speak out or hold your piece take the risk and see what happens. I think you will be pleasantly surprised.

"We are all children of God, of Spirit, and we inherit the grace and courage and wisdom of all who have come before. We have been given a precious and potent gift. We must reclaim the richness of being alive." Wayne Muller

LIVING A SPIRITUAL LIFE

There is a story about a man sitting by the road when a stranger asks him how to get to Mount Olympus, he responds "Just make every step you take go in that direction." In the spiritual arena, we reach higher and higher by changing our consciousness. Ernest Holmes puts it this way, "The greatest experience of our life is the conscious use of the God power within us; doing it we receive untold good."

Barbara De Angelis relates a story about a man on a plane who has the shade pulled almost all the way down. He is straining to look out the window through a four-inch section. He stayed craning his neck for the entire flight. How many of us live that way? We are willing to look at life through a small piece of consciousness and wonder why we feel confused or lost.

The Sufis tell us the world isn't our prison, our prison is our way of thinking. Earning a living and relationships don't make it difficult to find illumination, they are the road to finding it. One author refers to them as "Creative catalysts for spiritual evolution," the test lies in how we handle our day to day issues.

We teach that we become what we think. So, as we deepen our consciousness our life changes. We become more aware of Spirit expressing in and through our lives, and soon not only are we aware of it but other people see the change in us. The loving being we are becoming lights up our little corner of the world. What a gift, who could ask for more?

"Be lamps unto yourselves; be your own confidence, hold the truth within yourselves as the only truth." The Buddha

GOING THROUGH DIFFICULT TIMES

The spiritual journey is not about finding lasting peace. At some point we will all face challenging times. Real peace comes from within. Ernest Holmes writes, "Learn to see through confusion into peace, to see through sickness into health, to see through poverty into success and abundance, to believe in the all-sustaining good. Learn to trust in God and be at peace." When we do what Dr. Holmes is suggesting, we find a lasting peace that comes from our source. We find comfort knowing that Spirit is guiding us through the tough times and we are not alone.

There are many practices we can utilize to move beyond difficult times, talking to a minister or practitioner, meditation, prayer, using affirmations are all helpful. I would also recommend using your community. Research shows that people who chose to stay alone suffer more. In community you can ask for help. The chances are that someone in your community has had the same issue and can tell you how they got through their tough time. Their stories can inspire you to take action.

Grief can paralyze us with fear. Yet, it is also an opportunity to heal. Recently, Anderson Cooper was interviewing Stephen Colbert. It was several months after Anderson lost his mother. Colbert said that even events that we don't want are a gift. Cooper asked him if he meant it and Colbert said, "Yes because all of life is a gift." What a great thought to remember, in times of stress and pain.

"Too many of us are not living our dreams because we are living our fears." Les Brown

Embracing Change

Instead of fearing change we need to focus on how to make it work for us. Every loss, every difficulty provides us with an opportunity for growth if we are open to it. We get to work out our future. Life doesn't stay the same. Security is not secure. The risks we don't take now are the regrets we have later.

In a study done by Columbia University, researchers found that age had nothing to do with learning new things. No matter what age, people were able to learn shorthand and Russian. The only reason older people had difficulty is when they used age as an excuse.

In the movie *Defending Your Life* with Albert Brooks and Meryl Streep, people who die are put on trial to evaluate their lives. The trial is not to see if they led good or bad lives, but rather if they learned to conquer fear, that was the goal of life. If they did, they move on, if they didn't they go back. James Robinson reminds us, "Greatness in the last analysis is largely bravery; courage in escaping from old ideas and standards and respectable ways of doing things." In short, life works best when we step out of our comfort zone.

"I've learned silence from the talkative, tolerance from the intolerant, and kindness from the unkind. Yet, strange I am ungrateful to these teachers." Kahlil Gibran

CHANGE YOUR THINKING AND SEE THE RESULTS

Life meets our expectations. It is like a mirror of our consciousness. There is a wonderful story about a man sitting by the side of the road when a stranger who is moving to the man's town asks what the people there are like. The man asks the stranger what the people in his last town were like and he replies, "Cold and not kind." "The people in this town will be the same" is the response. A few minutes later another man comes and asks the same question. Once again, the man asks what the people in his previous town were like, "Wonderful, loving and kind, he replies. "I suspect that is what you will find here" is the reply. What we expect from life is what we get.

Ralph Waldo Emerson writes, "There is no planet, sun or star that could hold you, if you knew who you are." We are powerful spiritual beings. If you aren't sure where to begin to exercise your power be still and listen. Trust that the same power that began everything will guide you to the right road.

Wherever you are in life you can change what life is showing you by changing the pattern of your thinking. The change might not be instantaneous but it will happen. For every cause there is an effect. When we change the cause, we change the effect. As Jesus reminds us, "It is done unto you as you believe," very powerful words.

"The eye by which I see God is the same eye by which God sees me." Meister Eckhart

PURPOSE, POWER & PASSION

Someone once wrote, "The privilege of a lifetime is being who you are." We are not here by accident. We all have a purpose, we have a gift to offer, and since we are all unique so is our gift. If we don't share our gift it is lost forever. Sometimes sharing our gift can be scary, it means we have to leave our comfort zone. For years I felt I had more to offer but I also had responsibilities I let keep me trapped. When I finally, made the decision to take the risk my life completely changed. What appeared to be roadblocks fell away because of the passion and purpose I came to life with. As Dr. Holmes reminds us, "We need to enter into the game of life with zest and with an enthusiasm that overflows with life."

There is a story about a man who goes to see a monk to, learn about God. Nothing seems to sink in, so they go for a swim. The monk holds the man's head under water until he gasps for breath. He angrily asks, "Why did you do that?" The monk replies, "When you have the same passion for God as you did for your next breath you'll get it." When we approach life with joy and conviction life responds in kind.

I read an article about people with multiple personalities. When they are exhibiting one of their personalities, they may exhibit symptoms of a disease such as diabetes or asthma. When they move to another personality, they don't have the disease. That speaks to the power of our mind. Imagine what we can do when we harness that energy for positive results.

"It is your path and your road and yours alone; others can walk it with you, but no one can walk it for you." Rumi

LIVING IN UNCERTAIN TIMES

Two men were going for an evening walk when one pointed to a small hut and said the man who lives there has forsaken the world and lives only to find God. His friend thinks for a while and responds that he will only find God when he returns to the world and shares in everyone's joys and sorrows. Living our life isn't a barrier to spiritual growth; it is the path upon which it happens. The true test of our spirituality is how we live our daily life.

Life is synonymous with change. People are born and people die; that is the cycle of life. Our life can change on a dime. How we adjust, how we face emergencies are all opportunities to grow. Security is an illusion. The more we try to hold on the more we live in fear. We really live when we allow our life to unfold.

So often in our life when bad times pass, we realize they helped make us what we have become. We feel the pain and move beyond to greater opportunities. Ask yourself "when did a difficult time in your life turn out to be a gift?' Recently I asked that question to my congregation and almost everyone had a story. As Eckhart Tolle writes, "When you become comfortable with uncertainty, infinite possibilities open up in your life."

"Be kind for everyone you meet is fighting a great battle."
Philo

MOVING FROM FEAR TO FAITH

Lama Surya Das writes about the Tibetan word "Chod" which means "cutting through dualism." It is a practice based on the simple premise that cutting through our fears brings freedom and peace of mind, for instance sitting in a cemetery all night or spending the weekend riding the subway to overcome a fear of trains. It is like asking yourself, "What is my biggest fear? Who or what am I afraid of?" It is getting to know our fears on an intimate level and by doing so moving beyond them.

Rachel Remen tells of working with a cancer patient who could not find a safe place in a meditation she was using with him. No matter what he did nothing helped. Then he imagined himself a little boy in his mother's arms and that helped. After a while, he realized that the arms around him were his own, and that the place of safety was inside him, not outside where he had been looking. All of our safety zones are within where Spirit resides.

Looking without for guidance only leads to doubt and frustration. When we realize that what we have been searching for was right with us all the time, our life can take on new meaning and we are able to move to a place of peace and serenity. Or as we are reminded by Appolinaire, "Come to the edge, but it's too high. Come to the edge, but we might fall. Come to the edge, and so they came, and he pushed them, and they flew."

"Fear not. What is not real never was and never will be. What is real, always was, and cannot be destroyed."
The Bhagaved Gita

THE PEARL PRINCIPLE

In the Bible story below, the Pearl is the Christ, our true spiritual identity. It is the greatest truth of who we are. Once we recognize spiritual truth, we need to make it our own. We need to release any beliefs that no longer serve us and build a spiritual practice that enhances our new belief system.

The poet Robert Frost wrote, "Two roads diverged in a wood, and I took the one less traveled by. And that made all the difference." The road less traveled requires effort willingness to go where you never traveled before. It requires time and dedication, a need to change to do something different, to begin to see ourselves as a divine expression.

Arun Gandhi writes about his grandfather Mahatma Gandhi. He was not born the Mahatma. He once walked a very different path but he changed. He made an inner transformation. One has to work to become a Mahatma; just as anyone has to work to be transformed.

A salesman approached a farmer and tells him he has a book that will tell him everything he needs to know about farming. The book will tell him when to sow, when to reap, and all about the weather. The farmer listens and then tells the salesman, "Young man I know everything in the book. That's not my problem, my problem is doing it." Spirituality is about more than talking and doing. It means doing the work to experience life in a new way.

"The Kingdom of Heaven is like a merchant in search of fine pearls, who on finding one pearl of great value, went and sold all he had and bought it." Matthew 13:45-46

ANTICIPATION

Do you remember when you were a child, the sense of expectation you felt on this the day before Christmas? Either tonight or tomorrow we would get to open our presents and see what great surprises were in store for us.

As adults and students of Science of Mind we can see the truth of Dr. Holmes' words in the quote below. The gifts of heaven are available to us every day. They don't come just once a year. And they come to all of us, not just a special chosen few. Isn't that an even more marvelous gift? Anything you and I could ever hope for are ours right now just for the asking.

We also get to choose how to use the gifts of Spirit. In fact, we can choose not to use them. Perhaps the greatest gift of all is free choice. We can create the life we wish to have by simply saying yes to the One who created all that is. There is nothing to assemble, no warrantees to fill out, no ribbons to untie, and no worries about returns; there is only recognizing our oneness with Spirit and letting our good flow forth. Come to think of it perhaps Carly Simon was right when she wrote, "These are the good old days."

"To each is given what he needs and the gifts of heaven come alike to all. How we shall use these gifts is all that matters."
Ernest Holmes

CHRISTMAS UNWRAPPED

Ernest Holmes tells us this is a wonderful time of year. For us it isn't about the birth of a savior. We don't need to be saved. We honor the eternal birth of Spirit as the light of the world. It is for remembrance, not about lavish gifts. It is about the kind thought, the gentle act; it is giving our humanity to humanity. In Jesus we celebrate the symbolic birth of God in man, the incarnation of the living Spirit in you and me.

Jesus was born in a stable. The lesson here is that it shows we can find God anywhere. Our background is of no importance. It is what we do with it that matters. When Erin McCormick was thirteen, her parents told her the family was going to work at a homeless shelter on Christmas Eve. She threw a fit. When she walked in and saw 30 homeless men singing softly, her heart melted. One of the men thanked her and called her an angel. When she got home, this is the letter she wrote to Santa.

Dear Santa,

I wrote you a letter earlier, but I am writing a new one now. Please take care of the man I met earlier and bring him some of the gifts you were bringing me. Please keep him safe from the outdoors and make sure he is happy. That's all I want this year. You can still bring me presents but the one thing I want is for you to look out for my new friend.

Love Erin

That is the message of Christmas.

"What good is it to me if this eternal birth of the divine son takes place unceasingly but does not take place within myself?" Meister Eckhart

GETTING YOUR LIFE TO HUM

Ernest Holmes writes, "Life is a song let's sing it." I like that a lot. So, how can we live a larger more expansive life and allow Spirit to speak through us if we want our life to be a song? The answer is we need to develop the consciousness to invite that song in. Emerson tells us that if the stars came out once every hundred years we would look up and marvel at the incredible sight. But because they are out every night we hardly notice them. It's easy to lose sight of what's important and get caught up in day to day trivia.

A young couple moves into a new neighborhood and at breakfast the next morning the wife notices that the neighbors wash, which is hanging up in the backyard, is not clean. She says to her husband, "Maybe she needs to use better soap." This conversation happens several times, when one morning the neighbors wash is out and looking very clean and bright. The young woman comments to her husband that she must have changed her soap. He replies, "No I got up early today and washed our windows." That is how life is. What we see when we are watching others depends on the clarity with which we look.

Every day we can ask ourselves, "What brought me great joy today?" "Where was I most alive?" When we do ask, we find God shining through in the answers. I love how William James puts it, "These then are my last words to you. Be not afraid of life. Believe that life is worth living and your belief will help create the fact."

"What if we knew for certain that everything we're worried about today will work out fine? What if we knew the future would be good and we would have an abundance of resources and guidance to handle whatever comes our way? What if we knew everything was okay and we didn't have to worry about a thing? What would we do then? We'd be free to go and enjoy life." Melody Beattie

THE WAY OF THE MYSTIC

If most of us were asked to name a mystic we might say Jesus or the Buddha or Gandhi, and we would be correct. But how many of us would call out our own name or the name of one of our friends? We all have the potential to be mystics because divine intuition is in all of us. Ernest Holmes tells us when someone has a great thought or creates a great piece of art or a great piece of music these are simply signs that the veil is thin, the veil between us and Spirit. And if we do our spiritual work we can pierce the veil. He writes, "Know there is something more than law or intelligence we may come to for inspiration, for guidance, for direction, a power responding to us, a presence pressing against us, an animation flowing through us, a light within."

In the book, *The Power of Kabala*, Yahuda Berg discusses the 1% of reality and the 99% of reality. The 1% is our five senses; the 99% is what lies beyond our senses. The 99% reveals a world of perfection, a world that is centered in God. Here we act from a place of knowing, a place of peace, a place of Godliness.

Why then don't more people seem to get in touch with the divine and their mystical self? The answer is simple. Some people take more time to listen to that still small voice and as a result they become more receptive and more open to the divine. Why not make some room for Spirit to enter your life? Take some time every day to enter the silence and see the results. You may be pleasantly surprised.

"When you get serious about God, God will get serious about you." Michael Bernard Beckwith

HEALING AND PRAYER

Deepak Chopra tells of a time he knew a great healer. This person told him, "I can train you to do the work I do in a week." Deepak did not believe him. The fellow said, "Its simple, the only hard part is removing the belief you can't heal, when you remove it then you can do what I do." The reason he said that, is God works for everybody. When we believe we can do something we can. If we believe we can't then that is our truth. Ernest Holmes said, "Truth known is truth demonstrated." The truth we need to know is we are one in God.

Years ago, Duke University had a project they named, Project Mantra. They took a sampling of people who had surgery and half were prayed for and half were not. The people who were prayed for had significantly fewer side effects or events, and they healed faster. What a great example of the power of prayer.

What we believe in our deepest self is what brings about a healing. Our work in healing is to uncover the wholeness that is at the center of our being. We must develop a trust in a power greater than we are that is doing the work for us. When we reach that state of consciousness, healing takes place, because there are no impossible situations for God.

"The beautiful journey of today can only begin when we learn to let go of yesterday." Ashmirdhaya

LEAP OF FAITH

When we reach a crossroads in life, we all search for answers differently, Jesus paced in the garden, Joseph Campbell went to a cabin for five years, the Buddha sat under a tree, some of us meditate or pray, others listen to music, still others walk in nature. There is no one way. What is important is that we make some time to go deep within to seek our answers.

Several years ago, Anna Quindlen delivered a commencement address in which she advised the students that, "Each of you has a Jiminy Cricket, a conscience or a guide sitting on your shoulder. It is your best self, the one you can trust." Uncertainty is a part of life. In the end we must rely on our faith. When life hurts, that voice that Ms. Quindlen speaks about will never lead us astray.

God is always present in our lives. In order to experience Spirit, we must be willing to deepen our consciousness. We must be receptive to the truth that is within. We can talk about God, read about God, or hear about God, and we still will not feel God until we open our consciousness to the presence of God. Spirit is present where it is realized. As T.S. Eliot reminds us, "We shall not cease from exploration and the end of our exploring will be to arrive where we started and know the place for the first time."

"Every issue in life is determined not by external conditions and things, but by our consciousness." Joel Goldsmith

CENTERING IN TRUTH

Living in integrity means being true to ourselves, listening to our inner voice. It means more than talking about ideals, it means living them. Thich Nhat Hanh states it is one thing to say you want to be a doctor and another thing to become one. One is talk; the other is pursuing a course of study. He writes, "We enter a path of transformation when we begin to practice what we pronounce." We need to walk our talk.

There is a Hebrew story about a rabbi who gets to the gates of heaven and is not asked, "Why weren't you Moses or some other great healer" but is asked, "Why weren't you Zusa?" In other words, "Why weren't you who you were meant to be?" Sometimes it is very scary to stand up for what we believe. It isn't easy to follow our hearts when friends and family are telling us to follow another path. Yet, Shakespeare reminds when we are true to our self we can't be false to anyone. We face the world centered in truth, and when we do, we empower others to do the same.

Gandhi, Martin Luther King Jr., and Nelson Mandela were all ordinary people just like you and me, who responded to life in an extraordinary way. We too can live extraordinary lives when we think and act from a spiritual consciousness. Ashley Montagu puts it so well when he writes, "The way I change my life is to act as if I'm the person I want to be."

"Within me is the unborn possibility of limitless living. Mine is the privilege of giving birth to it." Eric Butterworth

A CALL TO RENEWAL

Years ago, John Niendorf wrote about the difference between renewal and problem solving. Problem solving he said was a short-term process. Renewal implies a deeper process of rejuvenation, refurbishing, and transformation. Renewal speaks to living a larger life and being open to newness, and remembering we do not have to do it alone, we are supported by spiritual forces. We have a spiritual guide that is always with us.

In his book, *Seasons of a Man's Life*, Daniel Levenson writes that a person's dream is his personal myth, where he is the central character, a would be hero engaged in a noble quest. The reward is not just fame or fortune it is living one's life to the fullest, and leaving one's mark on the world.

Rather than setting resolutions that will probably be broken before January ends, this year why not ask yourself some deep questions that could lead to real transformation. Some questions you might consider are "Who am I? What do I value? What do I want to do with the rest of my life? What is the first thing I can do to begin living my dreams?" As Joseph Campbell reminds us, "We must be willing to give up the life we've planned, so as to have the life that's waiting for us. The old skin has to be shed before the new one can come."

"Today I close the door to the past, open the door to the future, take a deep breath and step through, and start a new chapter in my life." Anonymous

THE POWER OF BELIEVING

In the Bible God tells Moses, "Take off your shoes, the place where you stand is holy ground." The same is true for us today. There is no holier ground than wherever you are right now. This is our time to create the life we want. We create with our consciousness. Ernest Holmes tells us, "Everything that ever comes to us comes from mind. Our minds are unlimited; if we can think it, we can create it."

Reverend Donald Curtis writes about a time he and his wife were on a fishing boat. The experienced fishermen laughed at their rented equipment. Soon however Bernice, caught one beautiful fish, then another, and then still another. The fishermen stopped laughing. When asked how she did it, Bernice replied, "I just visualize the fish swimming along and coming to my hook." She expected to catch a fish. We get what we expect from life. Expectancy is the cause of everything that happens in our life.

The only thing that holds us back is limiting beliefs. They cut us off from our innate wisdom. If you believe in lack you will always be short of money. Our belief creates the experience of our reality, and the good news is we can replace any belief. And when we change our beliefs, we change our life.

"The Kingdom of God cometh not with observation: Neither shall they say lo here or lo there for lo the Kingdom of God is within you." Jesus of Nazareth

GRADUATION

"Whether we graduate from a four-year course of study or a ten-week class, it is recognized that we have taken a big step, but it is not a measure of completion. It is, rather, a beginning. In the spiritual life, we must always be open to new ideas and ways of being. Ernest Holmes tells us there are no barriers to our greater good. As we use the principles of Science of Mind, we can go deeper and deeper, and, in effect, become as great as we will allow ourselves to be.

Spirit keeps whispering to us to keep moving along our divine path wherever it calls. There are times in my own journey when I felt as though I was being moved along in spite of myself. That "divine discontent" that we all experience is telling us that the learning never ends; there is always more to come.

Perhaps the two most important lessons we must learn are commitment and trust. Commitment to invest the time, energy, and effort that are required to become all we might be. Trust that whatever we are encountering is perfect, just the way it is, and is not.

Jennifer James wrote, "Success is not a destination that you ever reach. Success is the quality of the journey." We make our lives more vibrant by constantly reaching beyond our comfort zone. Sometimes the reaching is exhilarating. Sometimes it's terrifying, but it's always rewarding because, in the end, it's the vehicle that enables us to blossom into the person we are meant to become.

"And when you have reached the mountaintop, then you shall begin to climb." Kahlil Gibran

Illuminations

A Ring and a Prayer

Recently, my wife and I visited several jewelers to have our wedding bands resized. The results were dismaying. One jeweler wanted $800 and the other $600. Both figures were well beyond what we were expecting to pay.

We then found out that the price of gold closed at $1400 an ounce that day so we decided to sell the rings. Once again we were disappointed. Both jewelers made us offers well below what we were expecting to receive. So we were stumped, we couldn't really afford to have the rings resized and we were being offered less than a third of what we believed to be a fair price for the rings.

As we sat in our car trying to decide what our next step would be, my wife said, "Why don't we pray for guidance." So we did a treatment for divine guidance. We then began to drive home when Becky said, "There is a jeweler on the next block that I heard was an honest businessman, let's stop in his store," so we did. He offered us more money to sell them but he wondered why we weren't resizing them as they were quite unique. We told him resizing them was too expensive to which he said, "No it's not," and he made us an offer that was less than twenty percent of what the other jewelers offered. We are now once again proudly wearing our beautiful wedding bands.

What a wonderful reminder about the power of prayer. Here we were a minister and a practitioner emeritus both feeling very discouraged until one of us said, "Let's pray." And of course, it worked. Ernest Holmes writes, "We shall receive that for which we ask. It shall be opened for us when we knock, and we shall find that for which we are searching." We needed guidance and it came quickly.

It is easy to allow seeming obstacles and barriers to get us down and leave us feeling confused and doubtful. However, Ernest Holmes gave us a tool that enables us to rise above appearances and life's disappointments. So next time life is hurting take a moment to breathe and go within and touch that Divine Presence that resides in all of us. Do a treatment and know your prayer will be answered. Spirit cannot help but reward our faith. As we so often repeat, "God is good all the time."

BLESSINGS ABOUND

Ernest Holmes reminds us that, "There is an interior reality to everything. A divine pattern is hidden in everything." I am sure that for all of us there have been times when that divine pattern was very well hidden. In fact, we may have doubted it existed at all. I know I have been there. Yet somehow in all the pain and fear, we can trust that we are never alone. Spirit is always right there with us.

Jack Kornfield writes of the concept of Satori which is the first taste of enlightenment. He says we are all candidates for it. He recounts a story about someone struggling to figure out who he is and what he is doing when suddenly he sees very clearly that everything is all right just as it is. Blessings abound all around us and our task to be aware of them. When we seek to find Spirit in our lives, we encounter the blessings and we see that even in the difficult times good is all around us.

In my own experience, one of the greatest gifts I have is community. It is a place where I can go to be heard, accepted, loved and to share the hopes and dreams my wife and I have for our lives. It is somewhere where I can be myself, and in those times when the divine pattern is well hidden, I have friends who can remind me to look harder and I will find it. They help me to remember that everything happens for a reason and when one door closes another opens.

Recently, I read something put out by the Chopra Center about the Law of Giving and Receiving. The article spoke about making a commitment to taking steps we can make to live by the Law of Giving and Receiving. Here is the first step it mentions, "Wherever I go and whomever I encounter I will bring them a gift. It may be a compliment, a flower or a prayer. I will circulate joy, wealth, and affluence in my life and the life of others." What do you think our world would be like if we all made the commitment to live like this every day? I think if we did, we would be living our Global Heart Mission, and we would become aware of the blessings that are all around us.

FEELING ABUNDANT

A few weeks ago, several of us were discussing what it takes for us to feel abundant. As I thought about our conversation, it brought to mind an incident from my graduate school days. I was studying for my MBA when a fellow student asked me to have coffee with him. He wanted to talk about an interesting cab ride he had just taken. It seems he and another gentleman had both hailed a taxi and reached it at the same time, so they agreed to share the ride. The other gentleman was a senior executive at a large mid-town corporation. During the entire ride from mid-town Manhattan to lower Manhattan he was complaining to my friend that he made $50,000 a year but had so many bills he was always broke. He said he had never felt so poor in his life. What you need to know is in those days $50,000 was a great salary.

After he told me the story, my friend asked, "How can you earn that much money and feel poor?" I don't remember what I said then but I do know now how that is possible. Abundance is a state of mind; it's not about our bank account. Dr. Holmes reminds us that, "If one wishes to demonstrate prosperity, he must first have a consciousness of prosperity." You can have a bulging bank account but if you feel poor, you are poor. Dr. Holmes also wrote, "If we think poverty and lack, we are certainly creating them and causing them to be demonstrated in our experience."

Years ago, I had my own business and there were times when I felt concerned that I might be facing difficulties because clients were scarce. My wife, who is a practitioner, would remind me that my clients weren't my source, God was. When I centered myself, and remembered that, good things happened. We live in an abundant universe. Spirit wants all of us to partake in that abundance. As we release thoughts of lack and limitation and allow thoughts of prosperity and abundance to enter our consciousness, our life experience is enhanced.

This month take some time to look at your beliefs about abundance. What do you believe? Then ask what are you demonstrating? If all is well, that is great. If not, perhaps a visit to a practitioner would be a good idea. There is a world of good awaiting you, why not claim it?

GIVING THANKS

Meister Eckhart wrote, "If the only prayer you ever say in your entire life is thank you, it will be enough." Being grateful is a way of life. As we move through our days we can make the choice to face life with an attitude of gratitude, and when we do, every experience takes on new meaning. Even the tough times can be seen as learning opportunities.

We teach that what we put our attention on is what we will experience. So, when we make the decision to focus on what we have rather than what is lacking in our life, we can expect to manifest more good. Ernest Holmes reminds us, "An attitude of gratitude is most salutary, and bespeaks the realization that we are now in heaven."

In the Bible, when Jesus multiplied the loaves and fishes, he began his prayer by giving thanks. He wasn't saying, "Thank you for this little bit of food." He was giving thanks from a consciousness of gratitude because he knew that there is always enough. He chose to look beyond appearances and to put himself into the divine flow.

Years ago when I was in the school of ministry, a dear friend received the news that her husband had made his transition. The news came out of the blue, and she was in a place of deep despair and grief. Several months later I asked her how she got passed the first few weeks of pain. She told me that she made a gratitude list. Every night before she went to bed, she wrote down five things she was grateful for. She said, "After the first week I realized I had thirty-five things I could still be grateful for and it helped immensely."

We don't have to wait for a tragedy to make a gratitude list. Why not begin today? Every day write down five things you are grateful for and see what happens. My guess is you will be pleasantly surprised at how much good is flowing through your life.

IT REALLY WORKS

Several months ago, my wife and I had a discussion about how we could enhance our income. The next day I saw an advertisement for an online class that taught speakers how to market themselves in order to earn more money. The ad said if one signed up within the next three days he/she could save $500. Even with the discount, the class would be a stretch for us. Once again, we talked and agreed to set an intention, to pray and meditate to attract the money for the class within the next three days.

Two days later we had the money and I signed up for the class. As I write this I have almost completed the class and I already have four talks booked and two more pending. Once again, the principles we practice made a big difference in our lives. Reflecting back on the situation, I had to chuckle a bit as I thought how whenever I do the spiritual work, I get a wonderful result. Yet I still can move into doubt when what I perceive as a crisis develops. Years ago when I was studying to be a practitioner, I was going through a difficult time. I did a prayer treatment and had an immediate result. When I excitedly told our instructor she laughed and said, "Isn't it interesting how we study the principles so hard and when they work we act surprised?"

I know what we teach works. I also know we are all human, and there are times when doubt and fear will set in. Next time that happens remember Ernest Holmes taught that, "Our belief sets the limit to our demonstration of a principle which, of Itself, is without limit…. It is entirely a question of our own receptivity" So, have faith, do the work, and if you are having difficulty knowing your truth, see a practitioner or minister. The good you desire is ready to manifest, just know it's so and it will be.

LOOKING WITHIN

As I write this, the Powerball Lottery has just paid out over a billion dollars to several lucky people. My wife and I never play it but I must admit this time we bought several tickets. It was fun to fantasize about what we would do with that much money, alas it was only a dream. I read that some people were buying $300 to $500 worth of tickets and one group even pooled $35,000 on tickets.

While the fantasy was fun, I got into a serious conversation with several friends about how much money is enough and what would an authentically spiritual person do with such a windfall. We spoke about believing in a world that works for everyone – a desire to be a beneficial presence wherever we are, how we could become a force for good in our community, and how we could change lives.

Carl Jung wrote, "Who looks outside dreams, who looks inside awakes." Life often gives us opportunities to look within and ask who am I? What do I stand for? Contemplating winning the lottery was such a time for me. The dreaming was fun but the pausing to examine my life's meaning and what I really stand for was exhilarating. Going deep allowed me to examine my beliefs, by asking myself when circumstances change would I live from a place of authenticity, or from a place of shallowness and greed. I truly believe authenticity would carry the day.

Periodically taking time to examine our deepest held beliefs is a wonderful spiritual practice. We can look at what no longer serves us and see if new beliefs and values would be more appropriate for us. We can also reinforce what is working, so we can continue to live well. As Ernest Holmes reminds us, "To awaken oneself is to be healed, made prosperous, happy and satisfied."

OPENING TO OUR ABUNDANCE

Eric Butterworth once wrote that we are all living magnets. We draw to us the things, people, and circumstances that align with our consciousness. If we truly desire to live a life of abundance in all things we need to develop a consciousness that believes we live in a universe that is abundant, and we can claim our share of the good. Put quite simply our belief system creates our reality.

Wayne Dyer wrote, "Abundance is not something you acquire. It is something you tune into." What a concept. It speaks to the fact that prosperity is all around us, and all we need to do is open ourselves to it. Say yes to all of the wonders that surround us, and I do not just mean money or things, but the love, joy, beauty and compassion that are everywhere.

Ernest Holmes wrote that he considered this quote from Jesus a marvelous thought, "It is done unto you as you believe." Holmes said, we have no need to coerce it, just let it "operate through us." Holmes wrote, "When we consciously embody what we wish, we are drawn silently toward it."

Recently, I read an article by a group called the Abundance Project, the article spoke to five places we can find abundance, our relationships, our self, our health, our giving and nature. Abundance is wherever we seek it. All we need to do is seek and we shall find. If you are struggling with prosperity there are books and tapes on the topic, see a minister or practitioner. Just continue believing you are surrounded by great gifts from a loving Spirit that wants you to share in the bonanza.

One sure way to get in the flow is to begin being grateful. Every day before you go to sleep write down five things you have to be grateful for and see what happens. Perhaps then you will see how true these words from Lao Tzu are,

"Be content with what you have, rejoice in the way things are. When you realize there is nothing lacking, The whole world belongs to you."

QUIET TIME

As I was about to prepare this column I paused to take a look at my calendar. This week I have three conference calls, four meetings, a wedding rehearsal, a wedding, the deadline to prepare this column, I have to prepare two talks I am giving to two groups next week and prepare my Sunday message, and deal with the various day to day issues we all face. I know stress. After seeing the schedule the first thing I did was go and meditate for an hour.

It is so easy to let the world and its pressure move us off center. Fear and stress can not only impact our health but we can't make our best choices when we allow our minds to be cluttered with what might happen instead of focusing on what needs to be done.

Ernest Holmes reminds us, "Know that in this presence there is no tension, no struggle no fear, there is no sense of conflict." In other words, when we connect with the Divine Presence we find peace. So, when I feel like the world is falling on my head I seek a place where there is peace and serenity, a place where I can become grounded in Spirit. That is why when I felt overwhelmed by my calendar I meditated. I needed to reconnect with my divine center. What I did not need to do was become so paralyzed by fear I got nothing done.

Obviously, meditation is not the only refuge from the daily grind. The next time you need to step away and center yourself, do something that brings you closer to Spirit, meditate, listen to music, take a walk on the beach or in nature, exercise, take a yoga class. Do whatever allows you to step back and gain perspective. Remember you aren't in this alone, with every step you take Spirit walks with you offering to share the burden. Take advantage of the offer. Reflect on the words of Kabir, "When you really look for me, you will see me instantly- you will find me in the tiniest house of time."

REMEMBERING WHAT IS IMPORTANT

Ernest Holmes wrote, "When we learn to trust the Universe, we shall be happy, prosperous, and well." The trusting part doesn't always come easy to me and many people I know. It's not always easy to look beyond appearances or the situations life is showing us.

In the last several months my center has been struggling, my wife and I have had to move because the owners of the condo we were renting wanted to sell it, and all the stress has played havoc with my blood pressure. So, happy, prosperous, and well have seemed far off concepts. My wife (who is a practitioner) and I decided to sit down and look beyond appearances to see where the gifts were in our life. The answer became obvious very quickly.

We have a loving community that brings our philosophy to life. As our situation became known we received offers of prayer, people telling us about apartments to rent, offers to stay with people if the need arose, people willing to help us pack and move. In short, we were surrounded in love.

The title of this column is Practical Prosperity; recently I decided to look up the meaning of both words. Prosperity has several meanings, such as, ease, security, and wellbeing. Practical is defined as, "Concerned with actual doing rather than theory and ideas." During a very difficult period my wife and I were immersed in practical prosperity. We remembered that our life is filled with wonder, joy, beauty, and of course, each other. And our community stepped forward with caring and kindness in very real and practical ways. They made our philosophy come to life. It took some difficult days to remind us about all the good we have in our life.

I hope our lesson can be a reminder to all of you who are taking the time to read this. We are never alone. When times seem the bleakest, take a time out and look for what is working, what gifts are still in your life and how blessed you are. These words from Ernest Holmes always say it best, "God is always God. No matter what our emotional storm, or what our objective situation may be, there is always a something hidden in the inner being that has never been violated. We may stumble, but always there is that Eternal Voice, forever whispering within our ear, that thing which causes the eternal quest, that thing which forever sings and sings." When we listen we can always hear the tune it is whispering.

RESILIENCE

Did you ever have a day or a week when whatever you touched or encountered seemed off kilter. My wife and I had one of those weeks recently. In the space of three days our car was broken into and the entire roof needed to be replaced, I found out the price of a drug I was taking went from $40 a month to $269 a month, and my wife was notified her medical insurance would be increasing $61 per month. John Denver wrote a song whose lyrics go, "Some days are diamonds, some days are stones, sometimes the hard times won't leave me alone." I know what he meant.

And yet while the hard times may not leave me alone, a comforting thought is neither will Spirit. So, while at first our heads were spinning and I must admit some fear crept in, we were able to move beyond our initial concerns to a place of peace. How you ask? By remembering our spiritual practice and moving within to touch the Divine Presence that is always available to all of us.

While it may not be easy to do, we can turn from what the world is showing us and know the truth that resides within. In the most difficult of times we can experience peace, love, wholeness, serenity, and healing. Prayer and meditation are wonderful tools, as long as we remember to use them. Ernest Holmes tells us, "To desert the truth in the hour of need is to prove that we do not know the truth. When things look the worst that is the supreme moment to demonstrate, to ourselves, that there are no obstructions to the operation of truth." How comforting to know that whatever life is showing us there is a higher truth operating in our life.

And so, my wife and I took some deep breaths, and did our prayer and meditation work. What seemed like a never ending financial crisis was eased, and we moved on, reminding ourselves that whenever we bring Spirit into the equation life is good. So, as you are reading my words stop and remember you are a child of a loving God, who will answer your every need, all you need do is ask.

SEEING BEYOND APPEARANCES

As I write this, it is only several days since bombs exploded in Brussels, Iraq and Pakistan killing and maiming hundreds of people. One might ask what does this have to do with writing about prosperity? Let's look at what prosperity means. Eric Butterworth defines it as," Spiritual wellbeing, involving the whole experience of healing life, satisfying love, and abiding peace and harmony." He goes on to say, "Life is lived from within out. It is not what happens out there, but what we do or think about what happens." In other words prosperity is a state of mind.

It is very easy to become overwhelmed not just by world events but the reactions we see from politicians and news sources. Our job is to go deeper, to look beyond appearances. We will never create a world that works for everyone by reacting to what we see. We must hold the vision that each of us is a child of God, and that love will always overcome hate. And that while we may not be able to understand what life is expressing, divine perfection is at the core of all that is.

Our Global Heart Vision states, "We see a world free of homelessness, violence, war, hunger, separation, and disenfranchisement." When that day is here we will all be living prosperously. We will have created our own heaven on earth. As Religious Scientists, it is our task to hold this vision no matter what is expressing around us. We can do this by taking responsibility for our own thoughts, by knowing that "Heaven is within us, and we experience it to the degree we become conscious of it." We can pray, visualize, and meditate on creating a world where love and compassion express everywhere. We can move beyond the fear and anxiety and step into the knowingness that when we see a prosperous and healthy world, we will experience it.

As Ernest Holmes reminds us, "When the time comes that nothing goes forth from you other than that you would be glad to have return, then you will have reached your heaven." With dedication and commitment, we can do this.

STARTING OVER

Thirty years ago, I walked into a Religious Science Center for the first time. When I walked out I knew my life had changed but I was unsure why or how. Now thirty years later, I think I know the answers and what our philosophy has to offer anyone who is willing to do the work to live the life of their dreams.

So where do we begin? The great message that Jesus brought to us is that God loves us. Each and every one of us is important to the One who created all that is. We are precious to Spirit, and we have been given a gift to bring to the world. We are divine beings having a human experience. In the eyes of Spirit we are whole, perfect, and complete just as we are. And, as we move along our path in life, we have the ability to join forces with this powerful essence to co-create the life we choose to live. What this means is you and I are spiritual powerhouses.

So how does it work? Ernest Holmes tells us belief is the key. The only limits there are in life are the ones we create, because Spirit has no limits. As Holmes writes in speaking of Spirit, "It is ready to fill everything, because It is infinite. So, it is not a question of Its willingness, nor of Its ability. It is entirely a question of our own receptivity." In other words as we turn to Spirit, It turns to us. No one is refused, all prayer is answered.

We begin right where we are. Wherever you are right now is where you belong. It is your perfect place even if it doesn't feel like it. Another one of the great messages Jesus left us is, "It is done unto you as you believe." What we put out into the Universe is what we reap. So many of us have been taught that we are sinners, or we are not worthy of the finer things in life. Jesus came to say that is not true. We are divine, we are loved and we were put on this earth to thrive. So, if life feels wonder-filled that is great. If life hurts know it does not have to be that way. No matter what has come before, no matter how life hurts you can move beyond where you are. Spirit is not bound by precedent. As you change your beliefs, as you come to recognize you oneness with Spirit, and as you begin put new thoughts into the universe your life will transform.

There is more good news you don't have to do this alone. We have tools to help you realize the joy of life.

THE BOOK

Recently I asked my wife to order me a book on Amazon. The next day I asked her when it was coming and she said, "In about a week." I said, "That seems longer than usual," to which she replied "Oh I used a used book vendor on Amazon." My immediate response was, "I don't want a used book that someone else wrote in and underlined, I want a new book." After being assured that the book was as good as new I calmed down and waited. Yesterday the book came, and it was completely marked up and written in, so I sent it back. But that isn't the real point.

When I thought about it, I realized how one word conjured up pictures in my head and how once that happened my ideas were difficult to overcome. How often that happens in life. We have a preset idea of something and it's very difficult to erase it. Meister Eckhart said, "The spiritual life is not a process of addition, but one of subtraction." He is telling us among other things to shed beliefs that no longer serve, to shed ideas of lack and limitation, and to shed old doubts and fears. It is much easier said than done, but if we want to grow in our spirituality, we must do it.

How one might ask? We need to commit to a spiritual practice, of prayer, spending time in the silence, attending services, workshops, classes, and reading books that will enhance our consciousness. Once we begin, we find these practices are more fulfilling than anything we can do. Gradually the old gives way to the new and our life is transformed. We attract what we have been seeking. We release hope and substitute faith, we release anger and substitute forgiveness, and we release apathy and substitute love.

No matter where you are or what you are experiencing your life can be more. It may take time, work and dedication but the journey is well worth the effort. As Dr. Holmes reminds us, "To realize that God is ever present, ever available, is to know that all the wisdom, intelligence and power of the universe is right where you are. Your word is power when you know this. This is why everything in your life depends upon your belief – why it is done unto you as you believe. Change your belief and you can change your world."

The Gift of Stillness

Last Sunday after our service, my wife and I were at home relaxing in front of the television, when my cell phone rang. As I was speaking to the caller, two people began texting me, and within a minute our home phone began ringing. That is a lot of stimulation. We live in a world where it's often difficult to get quiet time to just "be" but we all need it.

As I write this, my center is facing some financial challenges which will require us to move to a smaller space. It is a very taxing time for our Leadership Council and me. While facing these issues it is very easy to get caught up in the fear, challenges, and busyness that can be a part of all this. Yet, to have the ability to make the best decisions, we must rise above appearances and be able to think clearly. That is where the gift of stillness enters.

What I have found is as I move into a quiet space and become still, I feel a sense of peace and comfort that replaces the fear and tension that I have been experiencing. In this state, I am able to make better decisions because my mind is clear and focused on the issues, and not on the uncomfortable emotions that accompany them. Stillness also enables me to be a better leader because my center sees me as a person following our principles and being centered rather than fear based.

So, the next time you are facing difficult issues, stop and become still. I prefer meditation but that isn't the only path to stillness. If it suits you, take a walk in nature or on the beach, or listen to music that inspires you. Do something that allows you to enter a place where you move beyond the mind chatter and you can just "be." If you are working with a group, the next time you meet begin the meeting with a minute or two of quiet time, it will set a tone for the entire meeting. Remember that the divine presence is wherever we are. To hear what It is telling us, we need to make room for Its voice to be heard.

THE GREATEST GIFT

Once again, the holiday season is upon us. A time to celebrate with those we love. This is the time of year we get to overeat and drink, sing our hearts out, and engage in the custom of exchanging presents. It can also be a time to reflect on our lives, take stock of where we have been, and where we are headed. In doing this, the one interesting question we may want to ask ourselves is, "What is the greatest gift I have received?"

Ernest Holmes tells us that, "To each is given what he needs and the gifts of heaven come to all alike." In other words none of us should be lacking for anything. Dr. Holmes also reminds us that if it is God's good pleasure to give us the Kingdom it should be our privilege to accept it. What does that mean? To me it means that abundance and prosperity are all around us, and they are ours for the taking. As each of us opens ourselves to receive, the gifts are freely given. Everywhere we look blessings abound.

One might ask, "If it is true that the gifts of heaven come to all alike, why do some of us appear to have less than others?" Before Spirit can give the gift we must learn how to receive. That is why affirmative prayer, visioning, meditation, and affirmations are so important. As we develop our consciousness, we are able to receive more of our share of the divine bounty. And there is more good news; it is never too late to begin. No matter what your life experiences have been, you can begin today, to live the life of your choice. Spirit awaits your decision.

So this holiday season amidst all the hoopla and partying, take some time to pause and go within. Call to mind all the great gifts you have been given, and make a gratitude list. Write down what you have to be thankful for, all the blessings that you have received. Review the list every month or so, and remember there is no end to the riches that God is willing to bestow on you. Just ask and it shall be given.

THE MOVE

Last week my center moved. This Sunday we will be having our first service at our new location. Finding this new site was a lesson in how keeping focused on "what might be" rather than bemoaning "what is" leads to doors opening that we never knew existed.

Our former location was affordable, but rather dark and many members found it unappealing, so our Sunday attendance was falling. When that happened our finances were also taking a hit. Yet, never once did our Board panic or move into fear. Each month we would recognize what our situation was, and then reaffirmed that the divinely perfect home was calling to us. And soon it did.

Several months ago, my wife and I were having lunch with a friend who is a Unity minister and is the spiritual director of a very large and attractive church. Out of the blue she asked us if we would like to share a part of her space, and she made the offer very appealing financially. That is how our move came about.

Ernest Holmes reminds us that, "Thoughts of lack manifest as limitation. Thoughts of abundance manifest as success and happiness." When we are going through difficult times it's not always easy to remember this, or to rise above thoughts of lack, but we can do it. We can train ourselves to think thoughts that are positive and affirming. It would have been very easy for my Board and me to see what was happening all around us and fall prey to negative thinking. But we did not, and as we affirmed that we knew our good would manifest, it did, because the Law has to respond to what we place in it.

We all go through difficult times, that is part of the human condition, but we need not wallow in our misery. Remember you are never alone, Spirit is always with you. Move beyond what you are seeing and know the best is yet to come. When I face difficult times it helps me to remember these words from Dr. Holmes, "Train yourself to think what you wish to think, be what you wish to be, feel what you wish to feel, and place no limit on Life."

THERE IS ALWAYS ENOUGH

I grew up in a family whose consciousness was firmly rooted in lack and limitation. Even though both my parents worked, which was rare in those days, I remember hearing conversations and arguments that revolved around never having enough money. No matter how much time they spent budgeting, and planning the household expenditures, fear and worry were the prevailing attitudes when it came to money. Yet, as I look back there was always enough. We had plenty to eat, in fact we often ate out at some very nice restaurants, we all had nice clothes, and we belonged to a lovely swim club. So, the real issue was not a lack of money, it was a poverty consciousness.

When my wife and I began studying Science of Mind, and I heard our minister say, "We live in an abundant universe," I loved the concept, but I must admit it took quite a while before I internalized it. My early lessons about lack and never having enough did not fade easily. As I learned to use the tools we teach such as spiritual mind treatment, meditation, visioning, and affirmations, my consciousness began to shift. I saw that as I practiced what I learned, no matter what I encountered, there always was enough, the universe did provide. In fact, most people who know my wife and I would describe us as risk takers. We aren't reckless but our faith in the ultimate goodness of the universe allows us to live in a way that is both exciting and fulfilling.

Several years ago, a friend provided me with an affirmation that helps me remain focused on the fact I am a child of God and as such should always expect the best. I was visiting a store that she and her husband owned, when she handed me a check for my center, in the space marked memo, she had neatly printed in all capital letters, AIMNSOB. I asked her what the letters meant and she said,

"Abundance Is MY Natural State of Being." What a wonderful reminder that everything we will ever need is always provided, we simply need to accept it and give thanks.

UNEXPECTED INCOME

For many years now at every center I have ministered to, we have practiced the ritual of unexpected income. In my current center on the second Sunday of every month we remind everyone the next week is unexpected income Sunday. We give examples such as you have a meal or go to a movie with a friend and they treat you, or you receive an unexpected refund on your taxes ... any situation where you receive money that comes into your life in an unexpected manner. Then on the third Sunday we invite people to come up and share their story with us as well as some of the unexpected income.

Throughout the years we have heard some incredible stories about how when we set an intention, Spirit always responds in wonderful ways. While the practice is a fun way to raise some extra income for the center, I think it has a much deeper purpose. It reminds us that our abundance is all around us. When we listen to the stories that people relate, we see that Spirit expresses in wondrous ways. And as we tune in to the beauty of the Universe, we are always rewarded. A second benefit of the practice is that we begin to look for our good. I know when unexpected income comes into our life, my wife and I quickly say to one another, "That's unexpected income." It's a great reminder that Spirit is always working in our lives.

Ernest Holmes reminds us that, "We should expect the best, and so live that the best may become a part of our experience." I think that's what we learn when we practice the principle of unexpected income. We expect it will happen and it does. We provide an opening for Spirit to express in our life. Dr. Holmes wrote, "We must trust the invisible, for it is the sole cause of the visible." When we believe that the Divine Presence will operate in our lives, we learn to trust and expect positive results and we are rewarded in kind.

As we approach the holiday season why not begin the practice and see what happens. Set the intention that this month and next unexpected income will appear in your life and see what happens. Watch how your faith will be rewarded. Think of it as an extra holiday present, one from the divine.

WE ARE MORE THAN OUR DIFFERENCES

Neil Diamond wrote a song titled, *"Beautiful Noise"*. In the song he pays homage to the sounds of New York City where one of the lyrics goes, "It's a beautiful noise made of joy and of strife, like a symphony played by the passing parade, it's the music of life." That music is made up of the many cultures, religions, and races that come together to form a city filled with a rich heritage of diversity.

I grew up in New York City, and I feel so blessed to have been exposed to its cultural diversity. We live in a time when some among us speak of separation and retreating into our own enclaves. Our world is fractured and in need of healing. When we can move beyond our fears and listen to people who are "different," we can enrich our boundaries and see new ways of approaching life.

Ernest Holmes taught, "The best way to make friends is to realize we meet Life in everyone. The God in us meets the God in others." Underlying all our apparent differences, we are all one with Spirit and each other. Jesus gives us a great example of this in the story of the Good Samaritan. We see two men from two very different cultures meeting under extreme circumstances, one has been robbed and beaten and the other comes to his aid, even though their tribes hate one another. The Samaritan is able to see through appearances and reach out in caring and compassion. That is what we are called to do today.

We prosper and lead a richer life when we grow as spiritual beings. We see opportunities to love rather than fear. We reach out with compassion rather than ignorance. We remember the two great commandments, to love God and our fellow man. Sometime this week seek out someone who is a different race, religion, culture or political persuasion and just be with them, with no agenda. Allow yourself to see how we are all so much more than our differences. As Nelsa Curbelo reminds us, "Everything in society tells us to distrust others. I think it's the other way around. We need to profoundly trust in those around us, in their potential and in who they are."

WILBUR

I consider myself an animal lover, well, maybe not all animals. My daughter has a pet pig, his name is Wilbur. She is crazy about him. She feeds him, lets him sleep with her, kisses him, and generally showers him with affection. I go visit and I see a rather homely animal with a mean disposition, who growls anytime anyone but my daughter goes near him. Recently I began to think is there a lesson here? I think there is.

My daughter is willing to go beyond Wilbur's surface appearance and see the beauty within him, in turn he responds in kind. I, meanwhile, respond to the outward manifestation and he responds the same way to me with growls and annoyance. Ernest Holmes writes, "We can so train our ears to listen to the Divine Harmony within, that we shall reproduce its melody, rhythm, and beauty in all our ways."

It works the same way with people when we are willing to look beyond surface appearances. We very often find that we have way more in common than we ever imagined. Last week I read about an elderly white woman who was eating alone in a restaurant when three young men of color entered. One of them approached her and asked if he could join her, she said yes and all four of them had a wonderful meal together. Now the three young men consider themselves her grandsons.

Ernest Holmes taught, "Love masters everything." So often we only read and hear news stories about hate and violence. The many small acts of kindness and compassion that occur around us all the time go seemingly unnoticed. But they don't go unnoticed by the people who are on the receiving end of loving acts. They help make a world that works for everyone.

In his book, *The Power of Kindness*, Piero Ferrucci writes, "It is up to us. It is a choice in the life of each of us to take the road of selfishness and abuse, or the way of solidarity and kindness." We are always at choice. So, next time you see someone who looks different, or who speaks differently, or who prays in a different way, take a moment to appreciate the abundance of diversity that exists all around us, and remember it is all God expressing. Who knows, maybe next time I go visit my daughter, I may even give Wilbur a hug.

YOU ARE A SPIRITUAL POWERHOUSE

Every once in a while, I tell my congregants that they are spiritual power houses. And almost every time I make the claim, someone comes up to me after the service and asks me if I meant it. Well I do.

We have the ability to partner with the creator of all that is and ever will be to live abundant and prosperous lives. It may take work, dedication, and perseverance on our part but it can be done. It is a matter of faith. When we believe in our own connection to Spirit and we release ideas of lack, limitation and fear, blessings abound.

Prosperity is a mindset. It is an attitude that moves us through life. Perhaps the late Mike Todd put it best when he said, "I've been broke many times, but I've never been poor." That is the attitude we need to cultivate. When we face life with a positive attitude we step into our power. We recognize we are the cause in our life, and we leave ideas of victimhood in the dust.

Think of how many lottery winners we read about that lost all their money within a short period of hitting the jackpot. It's because they did not have prosperity consciousness. On some level they did not feel they were worthy of such large sums. Ernest Holmes wrote about a salesman who no matter what territory his company gave him, he brought in the same sales figures. His consciousness was stuck on one level and that is what he produced. We can move beyond that. Expect that more good will come into your life all the time. There are no limits to what we can experience when we have the right belief system. The only limits to our greater good are the ones we create. Release the limits and experience a lifetime of joy.

I am a believer in affirmations. I find this one by Eric Butterworth to be particularly helpful in reminding me how Spirit and I are one. "I am a child of the universe, established eternally in the healing stream. I am strengthened, renewed, restored and made whole in every way."

YOU MAKE THE CHOICE

Yesterday I read a fable about a woman who comes out of her house and sees three old men with long white beards sitting in her yard. They looked hungry so she invites them in. They informed her they cannot come in until her husband returns from work. When he returns, once again she invites them in.

"We do not go into a house together," they reply. The woman asks why and one of the men tells her, "One of us is Wealth, another is Success and the third is Love. Go discuss with your husband which one of us you want to invite in."
The husband's first thought is to invite in Wealth. His wife disagrees and wants to invite in Success. Their daughter-in-law who was observing the conversation, quickly interrupted and said, "Why not invite in Love, then our home will be filled with Love."

They decide to follow the daughter-in-law's advice and invited in Love. As Love starts walking toward the house the other two get up and follow him. The lady of the house was surprised and asked, "I only invited in Love, why are all of you coming in?" The old men replied together, "If you had invited Wealth or Success the other two of us would have stayed out, but since you invited in Love, wherever he goes we go with him. Wherever there is Love, there is also Wealth and Success."

Ernest Holmes wrote, "Have enthusiasm and, above all, have a consciousness of love – a radiant feeling flowing through your consciousness at all times." When love is flowing through us we have wealth beyond measure and if we have that how can we not be a success? Many years ago while I was still in corporate life my position was going to be eliminated, and I was fearful we would lose our beautiful home.

One evening my wife asked me to sit down and have a chat. She said, "Ron I know you are upset about our finances, but when I moved to California I lived in a studio apartment. If I have to do that again I can. What matters is us. As long as we have one another we can face any challenge." That was the day I learned about the difference between Wealth, Success and Love.

WHAT WE WANT WANTS US

In New Thought we teach that God's will for our life is what we will for it as long as it does not hurt anyone else. Spirit wants to respond to us. Our job is to be patient and have faith. Jesus said if you ask for bread you won't receive a stone. Ernest Holmes wrote, "If you plant a rose bush you won't get a lemon tree." We receive what we ask for. Spirit returns to us what we put into the Law. It assumes we put it there because that is what we wish to experience. It rewards us by making our beliefs manifest.

If for some reason you are experiencing something you do not like, ask yourself what did I do to manifest this? What do I need to change? Remember it's not about blame, it's about taking responsibility. Recently, I saw a TV program where five youths entered a home to burglarize it. In the process the home owner killed one of the intruders. The other four were sentenced to long prison terms. Their moms were on the show and seemed to be pointing fingers at everyone but the young men. A former prosecutor pointed out that only the young men were responsible for what happened. Until we are willing to take responsibility for our actions, how can we bring change about in our lives?

Joel Goldsmith reminds us, that God is working out its life through us. So, when we desire a God experience, heaven will open itself up to deliver us every kind of good. In his book, *The Untethered Soul*, Michael Singer asks the question, "What if God looks at us as a mother looks at her child?" She sees only beauty and perfection. Wouldn't that God want you to have what you desire?

Affirmations

ONENESS

- In this moment, I recognize my connection to the whole. I am one with all. I honor all my brothers and sisters.

- Today, I honor the presence of Spirit in all people. I know there is one God in whom we live and move and have our being.

- Today, I release all judgments. I accept that we are all different, yet all divine. I know every time I look into the eyes of another I am seeing God expressing.

- In this moment, I seek the counsel of the God within. I know everything I seek is mine to find right where I am.

- Today, I search no more. I open myself to the divine within. I recognize I am one with the creator of all that is. I am at peace.

- I look for the gift in every situation. I know I am enough because the divine goes everywhere I go. I am surrounded by a loving creator.

- I am never alone. There is a loving, powerful presence with me wherever I am. I release all fear and doubt no matter what appearances may be, because my power resides within

LOVE

- Today I make a vow to walk through life expressing the love and compassion of Spirit. The love I receive lights the path I walk.

- Today, I reach out with love. I send love to people everywhere. I know that as I love, I am loved.

- Right now, I honor the love that created and sustains me. I feel it flow over me, and I allow it to flow from me. I am becoming the love I wish to experience.

- Today, I reach out and tell someone I love them. I make kindness and compassion a regular part of my life.

- Today, I spread love wherever I am. I love myself and everyone I meet.

- Today, I make the choice to love. I know I am creating a sacred space of healing, compassion, and caring.

- Today, I rejoice in the love of Spirit. I accept myself for all I am. I reach out in love and compassion to all of God's creation. I am filled with joy.

Choice

- Today I choose to open myself to Spirit. I affirm that all the good I seek is waiting to express in my life. I open my mind and my heart and know I am blessed.

- Today, I allow myself to feel the joy of opening to being more. I am calm and at ease. I step through the fear and let Spirit embrace.

- Today, as I move into the silence, I listen to the voice within and know that it is guiding me down my unfolding sacred path.

- Today, I recognize that I am in charge. I take responsibility for all I have created and remember I can manifest all I can envision.

- In this moment, I set the intention to make great choices. I am free and I use my freedom to create a life that celebrates my oneness with Spirit.

- In this moment, I relax into life. I know I am free to make choices that inspire and challenge me. I embrace all the possibilities that am offered.

- In this moment, I open myself to God. I choose to move beyond my comfort zone and step into all I can be. I release all negativity and accept that I am a powerful co-creator with Spirit. I am at peace.

COURAGE

- In this moment, I look within and see that I am all I need. I am one in Spirit, and that is enough. I am strong, I am secure, I am at peace.

- I take a moment to be still and listen. I hear the voice of Life and I allow myself to be led. I am at peace. I am where I belong.

- I move within and feel the power of Spirit embrace me. I trust, I accept, I move forward.

- Today, I allow the Spirit within to shine through all I do and say. I am open to ideas and ways of being. I allow myself to be reborn.

- Today, I release all old ideas that no longer serve me. I remember I am a child of God.

- Today, I step into the life I am meant to express. I move beyond all fear and know Spirit walks by my side.

- Today, I set the intention to live my life courageously. I honor the person I am and I invite the God within to express in all I say and do.

SACRED JOURNEY

- I trust, I commit, and I unfold into all I am meant to become. I am one with the universe.

- Right now, in this holy moment, I recognize my connection to Spirit. I allow love, peace, and serenity to wash over me. I am refreshed and renewed.

- Today, I go within and listen to that still quiet voice. I move through my life being true to myself, and knowing that as I do, I empower others to follow.

- I make a commitment to walk my path every day. I release doubt and fear and keep focused on the unfolding joy.

- In this moment, I know that all life is sacred. Every experience and every encounter is an opportunity to see God expressing, and I am grateful.

- Today, I commit to my own growth and development. I walk the path with conviction and dedication, knowing I do not walk alone.

- In this moment, I go within and remember that I am surrounded by the sacred. God is everywhere and so is holiness. I am blessed.

Power

- Right now, I know that I am a spiritual powerhouse. I make choices that lead me to a greater expression of life

- Today, I recognize the true power that I possess. I make the decision to live from the inside out, centered always in God.

- In this moment, I see myself as a powerful being. I am one with the Creator of all that is. My life is filled with possibilities.

- In this moment, I move into the stillness. I allow the peace and wisdom of an all-powerful Presence to sweep over me. All is well.

- Today, I step into my power. I recognize I am a child of God, and I step into life with confidence and gusto.

- Sitting in the silence, I release all thoughts of victimhood. I move beyond fear and step into my power.

- In this moment, I claim my power. I go within and touch the divine that awaits my recognition. Together we move forward to create the life of passion and purpose that is ours to live.

CHANGE

- Today, I accept that I am growing in spiritual awareness every moment of my life. I walk the never ending path of enlightenment and love.

- As I put aside limiting beliefs, I am reborn. I manifest all that I hold dear. My life is pure joy.

- Today, I know I am able to demonstrate what I can embody. I release old patterns and know new ways of being are mine now.

- In this moment, I commit to my spiritual practice. I go within and do my work, and know as I do, I change my life.

- Today, I continue along my divine path. I remember I am a work in progress, growing, changing and becoming more every day.

- Today, I move beyond old, limiting beliefs and open myself to new ways of being and experiencing life.

- In this moment, I know I am free. I set the course of my life. I choose my thoughts and concentrate on what I wish to experience.

FORGIVENESS AND HEALING

- Today, I remember wherever I am God is with me. We are one. I am healed.

- I release all anger, and the need for vengeance. I open my heart to the healing power of forgiveness. I am at peace.

- As I contemplate my oneness with Spirit I feel the connection more deeply, and my outer life is transformed. I clearly see that there are no limits.

- Right now, I release all anger, bitterness, and resentment. I see it dissolve into the nothingness. I replace it with love, compassion, and caring.

- In this moment, I forgive and move on. My load has become much lighter.

- Today, I move to a new place in consciousness. I release old limiting ideas and turn to new ways of being. I allow the healing to begin.

- In this moment, I release the anger and pain I have been holding in my heart. I forgive those who have hurt me, and I move forward to a life of joy and peace.

ADDITIONAL AFFIRMATIONS

- I am a divine child of God. I am Spirit expressing Its magnificence. I am Grateful for all I have to offer, and I share it with joy and enthusiasm.

- I move into the silence and listen to the inner voice of life. I follow where it leads; confident I am on a path of love and light.

- I know that with God, everything is possible. I pray knowing that, as I speak the words, it is done, for I am one with Spirit.

- Today, I begin to see myself in a new light. I recognize my spiritual perfection and I honor it. I let the past be the past, and I live right here in the present moment, knowing it is all good.

- In the stillness, I commit to remembering the law of circulation and practicing it. I give with an open heart and my good is abundantly and lovingly returned.

- I serve because I am blessed. As I serve, my blessings multiply. I stand in awe at the goodness of God.

- In this moment, I pause and reflect on how I am living my life. I rededicate myself to living to the fullest so, when my time is up there will be no regrets.

BIO OF REVEREND DOCTOR RON FOX

Reverend Dr. Ron Fox is an ordained minister with the Centers for Spiritual Living. He is a gifted speaker, and published author. His inspirational style, coupled with a keen sense of humor, make him a favorite with audiences everywhere he has spoken.

In 2018, the Centers for Spiritual Living honored him by designating him a Doctor of Divinity. In 2019, he was awarded the Meritorious Minister Award for his outstanding service.

Reverend Dr. Ron has been a motivational speaker and workshop facilitator for over 25 years. He had a long and successful career as a Human Resource Executive, working for such companies as General Foods, Glaxo SmithKline, Unum, and Mattel Toys. Ron also operated a very successful search firm in Southern California.

He resides in Port St. John, Florida with his wife Becky, who is an artist and graphic designer as well as a Practitioner Emeritus.

Reverend Dr. Ron is available for speaking and workshop presentations, and can be reached at revronfox@gmail.com or 321-474-2030.

www.ingramcontent.com/pod-product-compliance
Lightning Source LLC
Chambersburg PA
CBHW071727090426
42738CB00009B/1899